Leavers & Cleavers

Notes on an Old Recipe for Homemade Love

GARY L. RIGGINS

ARGYLE FOX
PUBLISHING

TABLE OF CONTENTS

Like everything good in my life,
this book belongs to Jodi.

PREFACE

LOVE **IS A COMPLICATED LITTLE** word that motivates much of our human behavior, both good and bad. Millions of people at every level of humanity have lived and died for this four-letter word. Wars have been waged between countries, communities, and families in the name of love, but that same word has simmered tensions and cooled human flare-ups. It is both a deadly serious and frivolous word, sometimes difficult—or at least awkward—to say, and at other times, a conversational byword.

Love can mean everything, or it can mean nothing.

Love led most wedded couples to the marriage altar, where they pledged themselves to one another "till death do us part." King Solomon, perhaps the wisest man who ever lived, wrote that "love is a seal upon thine heart . . . for love is strong as death . . ." (Song of Solomon 8:6). This book is an attempt to better understand this robust verb and part-time noun that joins two frail human hearts, calming some and making others beat faster.

Often with more passion than thought and usually on the fly, we talk as if love can be made, as in, "Let's make love." I've used that line in my own marriage to satisfy purely selfish, physical motives and expediency. After fifty-three years of married life—having loved and been loved completely—I've discovered there may be some truth in this passionate throwaway line. I've not figured it all out, but I have worked out a theory about how love might indeed be made in the full daylight of my senses with a steady heart rate and even breaths.

Gary L. Riggins | 9

This theory of how married love might be made is a notion I cribbed from the Scriptures, an old book on loving I've tried to organize my life around. As I understand it, God—the creator of all that is—wants a relationship with the creation. In trying to identify himself to humanity, he had his disciple John write, "God is love, and whoever abides in love abides in God, and God abides in him" (1 John 4:16). In essence, God and love are two equal sides of the same coin. If you know one, you know the other. Given that God is infinitely more complex than any of us can imagine, attempting to fully comprehend God or love is futile. However, that does not absolve us of the responsibility to seek a better understanding of God and a more practical sense of love, the strange word that joins us to each other and to God. Because the more we know about love, the stronger the possibility we might make more of it when our supply runs low or find the means to fix loving relationships that are unraveling before our eyes.

This book's general premise is that the Bible lays out the fundamentals of married love—a recipe, if you will. What unites marriage candidates is the solemn vow to leave all others, things, and comfortable customs and cleave only to this one (Genesis 2:24). For those willing to truly love another, love's ingredients of leaving and cleaving double as commands. These acts of the will suggest humans have at least some responsibility in the sacred act of making the kind of love that knits two human hearts together for a lifetime.

The cooking metaphor may help clarify the price, complications, and obligations of brewing up this powerful adhesive recognized as love. When the two complicated ingredients of a lasting love mix together with the right spices and are heated up, the resulting potion is the glue that sticks messy people together, come what may.

As most have figured out, the stuff that makes two people one is difficult to come by, and the ingredients—leaving and cleaving—are neither simple nor cheap. Though commanded, we rarely think about what it means to leave and cleave. Consequently, an examination of these two verbs and their demands is helpful. I propose a Behavior Model for Leaving and Cleaving that offers a course of action for leavers and cleavers and a way to identify and resolve problems that threaten long-term, faithful leaving and cleaving. The four biblical elements in this model—commitment, communication, understanding, and submission (specifically in that order)—are like yeast in a loaf of bread. They serve as catalysts, creating appropriate conditions in which love might rise. Added bonus: They are the antidote for any blight that would destroy it.

For love to endure through life's inevitable thick and thin, there must be a way forward, something lovers can do. Marital *love* is a verb, an act of the will rooted in two clear and demanding words: *leave* and *cleave*. Love is also a noun, the gooey substance that sticks men and women together "…till death do us part." At some point, we all have personal experiences with both the verb and noun forms of love. We see love do its good work—if not in our own lives, in the lives of those closest to us. We also know love's heartache and are changed by the indelible marks of joy and sorrow that loving another carves into our beings.

Like me, you have notes of love's effects on you through the years. Some notes are written on the back of envelopes, some are typed into a phone, but most are recorded only in memory. Our very personal observations are sketches of what happened and are colored by incomplete impressions, preferences, and timing that help us make sense of the world. This book is an attempt to make sense of an old recipe for homemade married love that's been around since Genesis. Hopefully, our uncommon personal experiences with love help us approach beloved Scriptures and tease out a better understanding of this mysterious stuff that holds us together.

We can never know it all. However, tempered by our experiences and guided by ancient divine words, I believe those who follow love's old recipe can make it.

Gary L. Riggins
October 31, 2024

INTRODUCTION

...not as though I were writing you a new commandment, but one
we have had from the beginning—that we love one another.
                                                    —II John v. 5 (ESV)

ACCORDING TO THE BEATLES, a bunch of romance novels, and my sinner friends in the balcony at the old downtown Bijou, love is something you make. They tell me that too often it's done in a great rush with emotions turned up to eleven, with little if any consideration of the consequences. Even less attention is given to the details of how love is made or how it may be sustained. Maybe the Beatles were right. It takes love to make love.

Calm down. This book isn't about the steamy passages in a cheap novel with a long-haired, shirtless man on a deserted beach gazing longingly at the sea. It's about the sometimes-boring process of making the sticky stuff that keeps ragged, imperfect human beings together over the long haul. That is not to deny that love is at times intense, scary, and absolutely the most fun way to curl your toes. It is all these things and more—much more. Love, in short, is one of God's greatest gifts, the *why* in so much of what we do every day.

Love for married folks is not a one-off event, something stumbled into, or a fleeting emotional connection. It is intentional, and like a fine meal, love takes preparation, time, and forethought. And yes, it is worth the wait.

That said, just because you like something does not mean you can make it. I like a slice of banana bread still steaming from the oven with a big blob of butter on top. Drizzle honey over it, and unseen choirs sing for joy. Much as I love this culinary treat, I can't make it. I tried, and I failed.

Last fall, my wife took our granddaughters shopping for school clothes. Overcome with a sense of hearth and home and inspired by the sappy family pictures on our homemade calendar, I decided to try something new: bake banana bread. After all, the five bananas that looked so appealing in the store a couple days earlier were beginning to look like a seventh-grade science experiment. The gang of fruit flies claiming the bananas for their own were a dead giveaway that something had to be done. Rather than throw out the bananas, I chose to try my hand at baking my favorite bread.

I soon learned two lessons:

1. There's no substitute for the real thing.

2. I am incapable of making the real thing.

One of the first rules of baking is to have all the ingredients on hand. I googled a recipe, and we had plenty of the principal ingredients. The recipe called for baking powder. I've seen Jodi put baking stuff away, and I know baking powder is white, so I got down the clear, unmarked plastic container full of white stuff. Then I dutifully measured out the ingredients, mashed the bananas, and warmed up the oven.

After mixing the ingredients and putting the carefully crafted loaves in the oven (these were big old bananas), I sat back and imagined how proud Jodi would be of me and how many points I'd score when she walked into the house to fresh, hot banana bread on the counter. I was almost overcome with my accomplishment until the oven timer went off.

When I removed the loaves, they appeared as flat as they were when they went in the oven. They had the consistency of my granddaughter's Play-Doh pizza and tasted only a tad better. When Jodi got home, she noticed the aroma of freshly baked banana bread (at least I got the smell right), but I couldn't get her to try a slice.

So, no—I'm not a chef. I'm not even a decent cook. Apparently, there's a difference between powdered sugar and baking powder. But in my defense, they're both white and fluffy. That said, ingredients matter. Even those with limited abilities, eyes, and taste buds can tell when things are done wrong and corners are cut. If I could distinguish between baking powder and powdered sugar or knew exactly where we kept each item, my kitchen experiment would have yielded different results, including more brownie points.

The good news is that this book isn't about banana bread, but something much more important. It's a book about marriage—your marriage, my marriage, and the marriage of your neighbors. This most intimate human relationship and its resulting families are the foundational bedrock of society. It is how we're held together and why we break apart. As politicians and preachers remind us, our communities, states, and nations are only as solid as these basic building blocks. Specifically, this book addresses the mysterious connective tissue, *love*, the reason most of us approach the altar to be united in holy matrimony.

Love is a little four-letter word that encapsulates a complicated emotion and a demanding verb that most of us, including me, don't fully understand. We whisper it in our most intimate moments and shout it out loud at ballgames, church houses, and concerts. However, not counting a slew of crude paperbacks, few books tackle the thorny issue of how love is made or cooked up in the first place. *Love*, a ubiquitous word that's so easy and so hard to say, is almost impossible to pin down. After enjoying love's peace and pleasure for more than five decades in my own marriage, I have a few hard-earned insights to share. Like a tasty pan of banana bread, there are a few fundamental ingredients that must be in the mix. After that, we're free to add special touches—raisins, nuts, cinnamon, etc.—that make this batch our own.

The Scriptures, that old cookbook for human flourishing, lays out two basic ingredients. This book will highlight those two fundamentals—leaving and cleaving—and tell you where I and many others shop for the freshest ingredients. Freshness matters, because when made from the right stuff, love fends off mold and rot and enjoys a long and lasting shelf life.

Consider this book a conversation between you and me, a discussion about something that profoundly impacts all of us. Granted, our conversation will be one-sided, as I will do most of the talking, but your experience in loving will come in handy. You came from a family and are probably married or know folks who are or who want to be. So, you have relevant experience to apply to the impending pages. You've seen good marriages and rotten ones and have opinions about how a union of two souls ought to work. Like me and millions of others, you have a vested interest in a successful personal relationship and know what it's like when it works. Please don't be bashful about sharing what you've learned.

Unfortunately, the time for ignoring such thoughts is over. You are, after all, reading my book, and I am a retired professor with too much time on my hands and access to a word processor; however, I need your patience. Inside and beyond the classroom, I've learned that we're more alike than different. For instance, neither of us wants to be embarrassed, made fun of, or treated as if we don't matter. Like you, I want to be a responsible and responsive marriage partner. I also want a decent shot at the good life for my children and grandchildren and to be viewed as a contributing member of my family and community. I suspect we also share the need to occasionally stand out from the crowd, to be recognized for our accomplishments. But then again, sometimes you and I desperately want to blend in, to be one of the gang. Oh, and we've both said things we wish we could take back and conversely, stayed quiet when we should have spoken.

I've had the honor of leading marriage retreats and counseling couples throughout the marriage relationship. To find something relevant to say, I made an extensive study of how marriage unions were originally conceived and explained in Scriptures. Many through the ages have organized the most personal and complicated mysteries of existence on the principles in the Bible. I have, and I started by reexamining what the old text had to say about this most intimate aspect of our lives.

While working on this book, I consulted original sources. I went back to the fount of all inspiration, a text older than most I read in graduate school. I prepared for an extensive search, but it didn't take long. Just a couple of pages into this ancient book, the *original* original source, it declared, "Therefore shall a man leave his father and his mother and shall cleave unto his wife: and they shall be one flesh" (Genesis 2:24). There it was, clear as a bell. Marriage was about two things—leaving and cleaving. If I could better understand these two deceptively simple notions, there was a good chance that I would know more about marriage.

Leavers and Cleavers, I decided, was a nice little package, complete with a catchy title and an even better outline. How hard could it be to build a presentation around this "brand new" concept? God already did the hard work of conceptualizing marriage and then squeezing it into less than two dozen letters. All I had to do was look for the fine print under each heading. But as my parents' and my own brushes with mortality taught me, nothing is as easy as it appears. (Exception: Making a fool of myself.) As the old saying goes, "It's a simple thing to be complex, and a complex thing to be simple." Marriage is indeed complex. After fifty-plus years of working on the husband role, I've concluded that marriage is anything but simple. The challenge is to find the simple truths hidden in this marvelous complexity.

This book is a culmination of over ten years of digging into the notions of leaving and cleaving and more importantly, their implications. Once uncovered, the truths under the rocks I kicked up in my research seem obvious and unsurprising. As my friends from the sixties would say, leaving and cleaving are "heavy concepts, man," thick with meaning. If they can be deciphered, they are the pass keys to a lifetime marriage. These two heavy but elegant words express exactly what serious life-time lovers do: leave comfortable homes ("let go") and cleave to the one they love ("hang on"). For at least two thousand years, the secrets to a happy marriage have been accessible to anyone with a hungry heart and a keen eye. They have been hiding in plain sight from the very beginning. Finding them was not difficult. Living them out is a different story.

This book is an attempt to capture this vision in words. My writing has been described by various editors and reviewers as "cheesy," "lighthearted," and sometimes "entertaining." The writing style is what it is, but that's not the most important thing. I hope my choice of nouns and verbs won't obscure the bigger picture of the seriousness and implications inherent in the topic. Marriage is perhaps God's greatest gift to fend off the cruel realities of an otherwise lonely and bleak existence. It is within this primary relationship that we learn of the bright promises in fully loving another.

I am aware that my own limited skills, experiences, and biases will find their way into every aspect of text, but I hope they will not be too distracting. Like me and my own faith journey, this book is a work in progress. As the old song suggests, I can assure you of only one thing: "We'll understand it better by and by."

Even when the instructions are on the counter in note form or neatly printed from the internet, cooking is a messy business. Sometimes, like my banana bread incident, we need a clear understanding of the fundamental process, a plain description of the ingredients, and insight regarding how to put all of it together, especially for those of us who are not chefs. As I hinted at earlier, I have divided my notes on love making into five sections. I've also attached an appendix with workshop exercises I've found useful in nurturing the fresh green shoots of love.

Essentially, this is my messy attempt to connect the dots that form the elegantly simple and beautifully complex biblical picture of marriage. I've talked about these concepts with audiences around the world and in my faculty office at Lee University with young people preparing to join hearts at the marriage altar. I've used these insights as a working model to counsel those whose marriages are in trouble and to propose adjustments that—in some cases—are successful. I've lived long enough to learn that marriages, like fingerprints, are personal and unique and that nothing short of the grace of God works all the time for everybody. I have collected and sorted through these experiences and tried to organize them in a meaningful way. My prayer is that what emerges from this project is a focused image of holy matrimony that calls each of us to a renewed commitment. If so, I will have answered the call to share the good news with as many people as possible.

With these caveats and understandings, here are some notes I've discovered on the ancient recipe for homemade love that has nourished relationships for millennia. It's best served warm—sometimes hot—and will keep lovers invigorated, neighbors talking, and the union of two lonely souls fresh and lively. I'm sure you will see things in my version of this recipe that might need to be tweaked or salted to taste. That's fine. Please do. And since we're now such good buddies, let me know how your batch turns out.

I believe the old Genesis writer gave us the fundamental ingredients for a fresh batch of love and left us with a little work to figure out some of the specifics. Not to be too dramatic, but there has never been a time when we needed more insights into the ancient art of lovemaking. Over time, various artists, poets, and prophets have offered their insights into the strange bonding agent introduced in Genesis. From the writings in ancient Sanskrit to the Song of Solomon, the collective wisdom in their poems and proverbs is that love wins in the end, for everyone everywhere.

Maybe you can use your own notes and add a few lyrics. The bottom line is that in a world starving for true, honest-to-goodness love, we are all obligated to try. Building stronger marriages and families is not only a biblical mandate, but it is also vital to sustaining our communities and our nation. Like so many things that matter and are deeply satisfying, the love that holds families together is always best when homemade.

Leavers & Cleavers

Section I

NOTES ON MARRIED LOVE'S FOUNDATIONS

Except the Lord build the house, they labor in vain that build it.
—Psalm 127:1

Overview

We jot down notes when we have a personal interest in learning something. Rarely are those notes perfect or complete. They're first impressions dashed off on a legal pad or outlined in a notebook, perhaps written in the margins of the text. Some of the most powerful and life-changing notes aren't even written down. Rather, they're quick mental notes concerning what worked or what didn't work in a given situation. We make notes when we know we will be accountable for remembering or learning a thing. In the early years of the last century, E.L. Thorndike found that even cats take decent mental notes when learning to escape painful situations or pursue pleasurable ones.

Human beings—and cats, apparently—constantly take notes to learn how to avoid embarrassing and painful situations (what not to say in polite company), repeat pleasurable ones (preferences on how a steak ought to be cooked), and succeed (learning the difference between a metaphor and a simile, especially if it's "on the test"). Such notes do not capture the full substance of a lecture or experiment verbatim, but they provide an impression of what was important to the notetaker. Often, members of a single study group preparing for the same exam have different takes on what was significant.

Notes help us adapt to situations large and small, important and relatively unimportant. They help us make connections between behaviors and their natural, logical consequences. For those paying attention, it doesn't take long to learn to avoid nouns (people, places, and things) that are harmful and seek out those that bring joy. As child psychologist Jean Piaget confirmed, adaptation equals intelligence. From our notes and subsequent choices, we learn to adapt to conditions, events, and circumstances. Therefore, people who are smarter may not have a stronger brain. They may just take better notes.

As we learn in school, notes tend to be very personal. You may not be able to make heads or tails of my scribbling on the Columbus's Impact lecture in our Western Civilization class. My style of notetaking suits me but may not make sense to you, as what is important to me may have no immediate value to you. As a result, study groups are invaluable. My understanding is enhanced when we combine our different views and challenge the thinking undergirding them. In these groups, a more nuanced and well-rounded version of events emerges. Likewise, these "notes" on marriage are mine, and like my Western Civ notes, they take on my specific style and emphases. Yours may differ in pattern and form, but I suspect when we combine our notes from our common class on marriage, we will find a lot of common ground.

In this section and the four that follow, I've included my notes on love—the mysterious substance that unites human hearts, its foundations, the two primary ingredients, and what I believe to be mixing instructions. You may struggle to make sense of my notes, scribbled as they were in the margins of an old recipe. If so, I refer you to the original recipe found in the first two pages of the Bible that describe the necessary conditions, ingredients, and instructions for binding human souls.

In our multicultural society, there is a wide variety of theological, philosophical, and cultural foundations that inform a range of views on this life-changing, "common" experience. As a man of faith, I have a clear bias on how messy it becomes when human beings are joined together till death do us part. As is clear from the title, this book comes from the Christian tradition and leans heavily on the Scriptures. However, as an educational psychologist, I know there is common ground across the wide-open expanse of human differences and opinions on how and why the red-letter day of marriage begins and ends. I'm not sure anyone can improve on the elegantly simple 3,000-year-old biblical advice on marriage—to leave everything and cleave to another (Genesis 2:24).

One of life's big lessons is that no one is perfect, not even believers. Over the long haul of leaving and cleaving, we make mistakes—we tend to forget or get lazy and neglect what the Apostle Paul called "these necessary things" (Acts 15:28). Things come undone. But marriage is a marathon in which blunders and short comings can be overcome. Even the best of us struggles and messes up even the marital advice to leave and cleave. But whatever your faith or cultural tradition, when considering marriage, it's vital to hear Jean Jaures's beautiful admonition, "From the altars of the past, let us take the fire and not the ashes." For those of us in the Christian movement, this translates to married believers being leavers and cleavers.

The Christian community is rightly concerned about the status of marriage in the United States. The good news is that some of the bad news is misleading. That is particularly so regarding statistical data claiming to reflect the health of marriage in our country (see Chapter 7 for details). Unfortunately, the deceptive bad news is widely and often cited in, of all places, the church. In my view, people of faith should be at the forefront in the battle to save and restore this sacred institution, and we should be its most ardent cheerleaders. We should be prepared to offer biblically based, vibrant how-to ideas that aid in strong, lasting marriages. It is necessary to be old-fashioned, to reexamine the original marriage model for insights that may have been lost in past and present generations. More importantly, we must teach our children the truth about the good news spelled out in marriage vows.

The Bible offers a beautiful word picture of how loving relationships ought to work, but like a puzzle box, it's up to you to find the pieces and fit them together, often with much trial and error. Without a clear idea of what the finished puzzle should look like, it's maddeningly difficult to find the right piece. Without that clear, full image as a guide, it is tempting to quit the process of sorting pieces and seeking solutions. Like frustrated sixth graders who can't get the notion of base ten, it's unfortunately common and natural to say, "This is stupid," and walk away. Successful students and spouses also get upset from time to time, but they persist because they know what picture will emerge when they put all the pieces together. As Solomon warned, "Without a vision, the people perish" (Proverbs 29:18).

Statistically, fifty percent of all marriages fail—within and without the church. Or so popular culture would have you believe. The truth is different altogether, and again, I will address this erroneous notion later in Chapter 7. But let's assume that half of all marriages do end in front of a judge. A fair question is, How do the remaining half end? There's only one option outside of the courtroom. It, too, involves officials in black, but they make their living selling vaults to grieving families. Either option—death or divorce—is traumatic, and will undoubtedly be emotionally gut wrenching. Why? Because it hurts when people who are joined together pull apart. There are no convenient dotted lines to tear one human from another. Consequently, marriage is serious business that either ends in death or divorce. However fun and exciting marriage is in the beginning, it always ends in grief. The good news is that in the seeds of leaving and cleaving is a design that binds fragile human hearts. If those seeds are deeply rooted and nurtured, the fruit will reduce the inevitable grief associated with marriage by at least half. Guaranteed.

In this section I share my notes on the foundation of married love. Even your brother-in-law knows that homes built on solid ground last longer. Ironically, before you build up, you must dig down (ask your brother-in-law). We'll burrow into the notions that undergird a solid marriage and examine the old idea that we are all connected, that life at its fullest is not a solo adventure. For those in a hurry, I'll offer my CliffsNotes on relationships (I got it down to less than a page). The what's-in-it-for-me crowd might like my take on the paradox of loving that describes how to get what you want in a marriage relationship.

To quell disappointment up front, we'll examine the debunked myths of Mr. and Mrs. Right that have sabotaged so many otherwise successful marriages. I've also included my own personal notes in another popular fable that love is something you can fall into or out of or is something you can't help yourself from experiencing. This section will wrap up with what I believe is the best news of all, your chances of finding happiness in a marital relationship. Spoiler alert: The statistical data strongly support the notion that most marriages will be wildly successful, even though the partner you've chosen may snore, have bad breath, or is otherwise less than perfect.

Together, my ragged notes offered in this section are attempts to better understand the foundational issues in making homemade, married love. While my personal observations may or may not help, I'm convinced that following the recipe in the old cookbook is critical. It has worked for millennia, sustaining life and love through the darkest of ages. Most of these ideas are neither new nor original with me. Before we had an alphabet, artists, poets, and songwriters tried to describe the mysterious, elusive stuff that holds us together. The iconic images painted on cave walls and canvasses, carved in stone and wood, and written in verse are strikingly beautiful, but fleeting. The love made following the old recipe by ordinary men and women remains stunningly vibrant and a source of an unspeakable joy that lasts "till death do us part." With these lofty promises and my limitations in telling this love story, let's get started.

Chapter 1

WE NEED EACH OTHER

No man is an island, entire of itself; every man is a piece of the continent, a part of the main. If a clod be washed away by the sea, Europe is the less, as well as if a promontory were, as well as if a manor of thy friends or of thine own were. Any man`s death diminishes me, because I am involved in mankind. And therefore never send to know for whom the bell tolls; it tolls for thee.
> —John Donne, *Devotions upon Emergent Occasions*

IN THE WINTER OF 1624, the sickly old pastor at Saint Paul's in London was deeply concerned with his flock's relationships with each other and their sovereign God. As funeral bells announced a fellow pilgrim's passing, the pastor dwelt on his own mortality. Students of history and theology know this poetic pastor was neither the first nor the last to remind us of the holy connection people have to each other and why relationships are vital. I suspect that at the end, in moments of clarity and quiet reflection, deep down we all know that "any man's death diminishes me." It doesn't take a giant leap of faith to know that this has significant implications for how we live. The awareness of the fundamental worth of human life is the foundation of our love for each other and our creator. As John Donne and countless other pastors have warned, relationships shape and define our lives, and they matter more than most suspect.

Human beings naturally seek the company of their own. The afternoon rush-hour traffic provides more than enough scientific and sociological data to make that point. The sheer number of people that choke the metropolitan centers around the globe is clear evidence of what anthropologists call *herd instinct*. We enjoy the company of those in creation that are most like us. The opposite pole, *social isolation*, is one of the most feared and damning sentences our penal system offers and is reserved for the very worst members of our society. Our longing for companionship is evident in every social stratum and in each phase of our existence. Even misery loves company.

People gather in droves to cheer their favorite teams, worship their God, and educate their young. As humans separate themselves into small clumps, the juiciest and most inviting topics of conversation revolve around how other human beings are connected. Our rituals reflect our need for connection. From the greeting, "How's the family?" to the salutation, "Goodbye "(a shortened version of 'God be with you'), we're intimately concerned with relationships. We seem to have an insatiable curiosity about the fundamentals of relationships. Those who have the latest scoop on who's seeing whom are sought out at parties and are phone companies' favorite customers.

Even though relationships fascinate and entertain us, there is a much more important and fundamental element in our attraction to each other. Primary relationships are the spiritual center of our lives, our home base. It is there that we rest and recuperate from the "slings and arrows of outrageous fortune." It is from this solid foundation that careers launch. It is in our primary relationships that we spawn and nurture other, more vulnerable lives. It is in our relationships that life happens—the good, the bad, and the ugly. It is where we live, literally. For those paying attention, the admonition of the Psalmist is crucial in getting our relationship houses in order. He writes, "except the Lord build the house, they labor in vain that build it" (Psalm 127:1).

As I read in the Scriptures, the Almighty doesn't build a lot of single dwelling units. He specializes in places where his messy children can live, learn, and work together, a physical location in which they work out their own salvation (Philippians 2:12). At the end of the day, when the bell tolls—as it surely will for each of us—my prayer is like that of the old pastor, may there be no one left living as an island.

Chapter 2

SCRIPTURAL CLIFFSNOTES ON RELATIONSHIPS

"Thou shalt love the Lord thy God with all thy heart, and with all thy soul, and with all thy mind. . . . Thou shalt love thy neighbor as thyself. On these two commandments hang all the law and prophets."
—Matthew 22:37, 39–40

IT SEEMS OUR INSTINCT FOR relationships was hardwired from the very beginning. The need to seek and find each other and enjoy the seeking and finding experience seem all too natural. Early on, the ultimate authority on the subject, the Lord God, declared, "It is not good that man should be alone . . ." (Genesis 2:18). He then set about making someone to be with the man, someone to whom the man can relate. In the midst of the beauty and serenity of the exquisite garden, Adam needed something else to complete him—someone like him. He needed a being with muscle and bone and dreams and desires, someone who knew what it was like to not know everything, someone who guessed, someone as limited as he. What was missing was someone with whom he could expose his own vulnerabilities, a partner to whom he could give his human self, and in giving, more clearly define himself.

He got more than he bargained for. While he enjoyed Eve's company, the price tag on this and all subsequent human relationships was high. And so it has been ever since. All working relationships come with benefits and costs. As mothers are quick to warn their children, there is no privilege without responsibility. We draw widely and often from our human connections, but there is always a price tag. And we pay—often gladly, sometimes reluctantly. We can't afford not to. Because the price of withdrawing from relationships is even greater.

Whatever price or benefit human relationships cost or offer, there is a deeper need rattling around in our empty hearts. Its nagging echoes betray an emptiness that the most satisfying human relationship cannot fill. It is a strong need to connect to and be defined by a relationship with the Creator. This is the reason Christ broke into history 2,000 years ago. He knew that we are largely defined by and our existence valued on the quality of our relationships. In the opening book of the New Testament, Jesus makes the point clear (Matthew 22). After a long day of verbally jousting with theologians about everything from marriage to taxes, an up-and-coming young attorney decked out in a designer turban went straight to the point. With the slight smirk that comes with too much learning, he said something like, "Sir, I've heard you speak, but my colleagues and I would really like to know your take on the 'law.' I mean, what's *really* important here?"

Without blinking, Jesus eyed his young inquisitor, took a deep breath, and calmly replied, "Just two things. Number one, love God. Number two, love your neighbor." As if to drive the point home, he added a postscript. "It is on these two premises that all of the law rests." Even the lawyer understood that the fundamentals of the gospel were ultimately reduced to the quality of one's relationships with his creator and neighbor. With his P.S., the Master indicated that every letter and every syllable in all the Scripture are about relationship.

All biblical characters and the interesting things that happened to them are instructive in how we should and should not relate to others. They tell what we can and cannot do, where the boundaries lie. They demonstrate behaviors that nurture and behaviors that strain the tender bonds that bind us to each other. Most of all, they guide us on our quest to establish a vital connection to the Almighty.

These biblical accounts of real men and women address the most basic relationship questions.

What happens when you do it right?

What are the consequences of doing it wrong?

How do you do it right?

What should you avoid?

Who are some of the people who got it right?

Who messed it up?

What happened to them?

These are follow-up questions the young lawyer should have seen coming. Christianity is about establishing, structuring, and nurturing relationships—first with our Maker and then with those who are like us, deeply flawed and scarred by sin. This brief passage in Matthew (22:37–39) is a scriptural *CliffsNotes* for those who can't read the entire 976 pages (this will definitely be on the test). In less than a single paragraph, Jesus sums up the matter. The essence of Christianity is a spirited and vibrant relationship with the God of the universe and effective relationships with our neighbors.

Chapter 3

THE PARADOX OF LOVING

"Give and it shall be given unto you . . . For with the same measure . . . it shall be measured to you again."

—Luke 6:38

A *PARADOX* IS A STATEMENT or proposition that, when first heard, seems to make no sense. It sounds contradictory, or like just plain "hooey," as my daddy would say. However, when the statement or proposition undergoes close examination, it makes good sense. The Scripture is full of paradoxical statements. Perhaps that's why some find little use in the fantastic claims of the gospel writers, claims that make no sense to the so-called enlightened of our age. Several passages, many of them printed in red ink, sound a little crazy, or at least upside-down. Case in point: The way to find the most precious of things is to lose it (Matthew 16:25); if you want to be first, be last and vice versa (Matthew 20:16); and the way to get stuff is to give exactly what you want away (Luke 6:38). These are all contradictory, at least to those who have not tried them out in real life. Those who have tested these crazy hypotheses in the field, even on a limited basis, testify of their primary truths. These paradoxical ideas are also effective in our most private and primary relationships.

Given the weighty importance of relationships in Scripture, it seems fitting that a biblical provision exist to aid in the practice of this essential art. Happily, there is. The fundamental concept is introduced early, barely two chapters into the Bible. After God hinted that being alone, even in paradise, is pretty hard, he fashioned the man a partner, a softer and gentler version of the species. In an elaborate ceremony with everything except the rented tux, God presented his creation to the lonely man. Adam immediately recognized a difference between himself and this new creature. He also recognized very important similarities. Reportedly, he said she was "bone of my bone, and flesh of my flesh" (Genesis 2:23).

Though some of the juicer details of this first marriage ceremony are unclear, what happened next set the tone for the most basic of human relationships for the rest of history. The officiant in this solemn ceremony declared, "Therefore shall a man leave his father and mother and cleave unto his wife: and they shall be one flesh" (Genesis 2:24). Contained in that ancient and deceptively short declaration are the two necessary ingredients in the marriage contract, leaving and cleaving—in that order.

In this most primary of human relationships we try out the fancy-dancy Christian concepts of kindness, gentleness, and meekness, among others. The entire fruit basket of these lovely traits is often memorized in Sunday School and forgotten by the Monday morning alarm. When learned only from the neck up, they are lifeless and empty platitudes hijacked by sentimental greeting card companies. Taken seriously, they radiate life, providing nutrients that feed living relationships. To really learn the high principles of Christianity is to watch them come alive in the mysterious bonds that knit human beings with each other and God.

Of course, the ultimate learning experience is to test-drive these high-brow Christian ideas in your own relationships with your neighbors and God. Indeed, forgiveness, faith, long-suffering, trust, kindness, and patience have little meaning outside of a relationship. Until they are practiced and experienced up close and personal, they are little more than pleasing combinations of vowels and consonants, lacking both form and substance. However, they bristle with life as you apply each in the crafting and nurturing of relationships.

These God-given fruits have deeper significance that remains somewhat mysterious to those on both sides of the giving equation. Dumping a truckload of undeserved kindness or other spiritual fruit definitely has a payoff. Although it appears a one-sided exchange to the unwashed, it is not. The "What's in it for me?" crowd has trouble with this basic biblical doctrine. This is because to the natural eyes, the one on the receiving end of one of Christ's gentle ambassadors seems to be the clear winner. However, another of the gospel's seeming paradoxes states that, "Giving good gets good." Ironically, it seems to work best when neither giver nor receiver expect it. Surprises are fun, aren't they?

The mysterious fun begins in your own neighborhood. After admonishing his followers to love God and then treat their neighbors as they want to be treated, Jesus calls his disciples to the ultimate sacrifice. He tells them to show love for the other through a willingness to die, "to lay down your life for your friend" (John 15:13).

From where I sit, that sounds peculiar. I'm called to build lasting relationships with God and my neighbors. Next, I'm asked to measure the strength of my relationship with my neighbors by the love I have for myself. Then, I'm called to give up that love for myself—all of it—for my neighbor and even to die for my neighbor. That price tag is a little stiff, but as stated previously, effective working relationships are not cheap. That paradox was not lost on the disciples. At least one disciple found the cost prohibitive and walked away. Love is expensive.

A careful cost-benefit analysis of the sacrificial love we're called to requires some explanation. In my own life, I am a better person when I practice those old Sunday School concepts that reflect God's love. In those fleeting times when I love deeply, it is easier to be honest and give away pieces of my most prized possession—the real me. Those portions of my life that I summoned the courage to completely surrender to the Savior are unexplainably enriched and returned to me ten-fold.

Ashamedly, I'm not always anxious to pay the high cost of loving relationships. To surrender my body and time and energy, my most prized possessions, on a blood-stained altar is tough. As even the most courageous notice, the trouble with a living sacrifice is that it tends to crawl off the altar from time to time. Loving requires hard work, patience, and sheer nerve. I have the good fortune of a patient and loving God and, for the most part, understanding neighbors. With his help and their patience, I'm being redeemed.

This fundamental truth—that I will always get back more than I give—is played out regularly and in great detail in my own marriage. The better I treat my wife, who is my closest neighbor, the deeper and more intensely she insists on loving me. In this exchange, I always get more than I gave. Acts of kindness, either random or planned, are never equally balanced against the willingness to lay down your life for another. But whether or not those good deeds are returned in kind, when I give away gentleness or other fruits of the Spirit, my life is immeasurably enriched. I am a better person when I love deeply and give without expectation or exception.

Within my marital relationship with my wife I have opportunities every day to practice my Christianity. Between you and me, what keeps me going is that our exchanges seem heavily tilted in my favor. I get more than I give every time. It's almost unfair—no, it *is* unfair. Yet, my wife never relents in her love for me. So, I keep moving forward in this relationship laboratory, where I get to practice this strange and wonderful notion of sacrificial loving. I don't always get it right, but in the lab, nothing works every time.

CHAPTER 4

THE MYTH OF MR. AND MISS RIGHT

"You're not perfect. . . . She's isn't perfect either. But the question is whether or not you're perfect for each other."
—Robin Williams as Sean, *Good Will Hunting*

TWO OF THE MOST SOUGHT-AFTER mythical figures of our day are Mr. and Miss Right. The popular thinking is that there's a marriage partner out there that's perfect for you. He is tall, dark, and handsome, or she is slim, smart, and plays the piano. There have been several reported sightings in and around malls, at sporting events, and on the front pews of churches across the country. Some even claim to have photographic proof of this mythical creature's existence. But like Big Foot, there are no live specimens currently in captivity. Nonetheless, many of us breathlessly hope the daring and handsome Mr. Right and the flawlessly beautiful and talented Miss Right will jump off the pages of a romantic novel and into our mundane and ordinary lives. After all, we deserve the perfect person, right? Wrong! Perfection does not characterize anybody at the marriage altar, the two candidates, or the officiant.

Unfortunately, the illusion of perfectness has poisoned the wells from which we weary, parched pilgrims quench our thirst for relationship. For those who look to the Scripture for consolation, one of the most popular places of comfort are the writings of David. He is real, almost too real. He knows what it is to be bone dry and lonely. He has been there, done that, and repented in sackcloth and ashes. He even wrote a song about it, Psalm 103. The catchy opening line, "Bless the Lord, oh my soul; and all that is with in me, bless his holy name" (Psalm 103:1) is sung in churches across America every Sunday. A few lines later, David explains why he reveres the Lord. David states that he is the one "who forgiveth all thine iniquities; who healeth all thy diseases . . . who redeemeth thy life from destruction . . ." (Psalm 103:3–4). A little deeper into the song, a grateful David gets to the punch line when he reminds us that "He has not dealt with us after our sins; nor rewarded us according to our iniquities. . . . For he knoweth our frame and remembers that we are dust" (Psalm 103:14).

In rough summary, the Lord does not treat me like I ought to be treated. Why? Because he knows I am truly limited, a "dirtbag" to borrow Clint Eastwood's descriptive if ineloquent phrase. Yet, I carry the treasure of the gospel around in this dirty earthen vessel. Like all vessels of clay, my personal bag has impurities and leaks and must be continually refilled. Don't judge me though. I share this condition with all my fellow passengers on planet Earth. My wife, my children, my mama, and even the clerk down at the 7-11—we're all in the same sorry fix. Alone, none of us can claim a perfect body, mind, or soul. We are all cracked and flawed in one sense or another.

The late Leonard Cohen, a Canadian poet and songwriter, wrestled with the big questions of existence and the uncomfortable reality of our obvious limitations. He clearly acknowledged our shortcomings and imperfections but embraced them. He suggested the cracks in our polished veneer serve a purifying purpose. They are the way the cleansing, disinfecting light of love gets into our souls. Those who insist on perfection in themselves or others will forever be frustrated in their search for a fitting offering to present to their intended at the marriage altar.

This is obviously troubling to those in search of the perfect mate. The truth that each of us is less than perfect is hard to swallow. It's a doctrine that's a little too hard for the soft-headed. We like to believe otherwise and perpetuate the myth of perfection. The media has learned that using the Big Lie that we're perfect or can achieve perfection sells everything from soap to socks, beer to bathing suits, caviar to Corvettes. "After all," the old Clairol ads suggests, "I'm worth it."

In the June 17, 1996, issue of *U.S. News & World Report*, John Leo called this attitude the "civic religion" in his editorial, "Let's Lower Our Self-Esteem." He identified reputable scientific studies that found no evidence linking self-esteem and school performance, and a strong correlation between high self-esteem and violence and gang activity. Instead of building upon Leo's work, the current professional literature aims to dismantle anything that threatens our love affair with self-esteem. As a result, we've raised generations of children who believe and then frantically try to live out the old Clairol commercial line.

The cult of self-esteem has invaded our schools and churches, weaving deep into the fabric of our national psyche. The cries of the Me First Generation have frayed our garment of commonality and threaten the foundations on which it rests: our marriages and families. Since this is a book on marriage, I will leave the school problems for another time and point out some possible ways that this psychic boosterism taints the soil that grows healthy families.

I recently spoke to a state-wide gathering of Christian young people. Beforehand, the leader told me that the reason most young Christians struggle with commitment to Christ is a lack of self-esteem. He wanted to replace the haunting feeling that we are woefully incomplete with the more acceptable notion that we are worthwhile. He stated that the mantra for this new generation is shouted in big letters on posters and bumper stickers that proclaim our deepest wish: "God does not make junk!"

Honored and excited to get a crack at impressionable young minds, I consulted my Bible to find scriptural support for what appeared a legitimate and reasonable biblical conclusion. What I found shocked and changed me forever. I did not find self-esteem. I found repeated warnings and admonitions in the Scripture to not think of my self more highly than I ought (Romans 12:3). I also found disturbing concepts that are not likely to show up on bumper stickers—old-fashioned ideas like self-denial, prefer your brother, walk the extra mile, and do your good in secret.

None of these seemed like popular topics for a youth conference, where the participants were victims of low self-esteem. How could I square the poster and bumper sticker with Scripture? The great line that "God does not make junk" is true. Unfortunately, it gets twisted into a license to behave in selfish ways that belie the cost of discipleship. It gets invoked to excuse a wide range of egotistical behaviors that run counter to the Christian lifestyle. While the fundamental message is true, God has witnessed each of us make messes of our own lives through stupid and selfish decisions. God may not make junk, but we certainly do.

In the end, we are pitifully inadequate. We cannot hold one little second in our hand, stop the slightest breeze from blowing, or keep the tiniest cell from aging. However, we can decide to whom or what and how we will give our lives away. We can desperately hold on to popular delusions of grandeur or—like Elsa, "Let it go." The Scripture and my personal experience testify that letting go or "taking the road less traveled" is a much sounder choice. This paradox, losing your life to find it (Matthew 16:25), is confusing to the Me First Generation and every other generation, but it's true. The sure-fire way to really lose your life, is to hang on to it with clenched fist. And the way to keep it is to give it away.

So, Mr. and Miss Right are not perfect and never have been. We made them up. For a comparison, go to the mirror and look at the imperfect person looking back at you—there are lumps out of place, the beginnings of lines that betray your age, and imperfections that a clever outfit can't hide. You know this. Others don't. Imagine that somewhere on this tiny planet someone thinks you may be the perfect marriage candidate. You know that person doesn't see what you saw in the mirror. At the same time, you've not seen the other person clearly in the mirror. Matt Damon and Ben Affleck got it about right in *Good Will Hunting*.

You're not perfect. . . . She's isn't perfect either. But the question is whether or not you're perfect for each other.

Chapter 5

LOVE IS NOT A GAME OF CHANCE

Love is a teacher, but one must know how to acquire it, for it is difficult to acquire, it is dearly bought by long work over a long time, for one ought to love not for a chance moment, but for all time.

—Fyodor Dostoevsky, *The Brothers Karamazov*

SOMEHOW, WE DEVELOPED THE NOTION that love is so mysterious and unpredictable that it sneaks up on you in the cab of your pickup truck on moonlit nights, in dark corners of the theater, or maybe at the park during an afternoon picnic. Songs, movies, and romance novels would have us believe we have little to no control over whom or what we love. In this model, love is fickle, almost make believe. Like fairies, love flits in and out of our lives, sometimes without our knowing, and leaves us baffled and awestruck. Real men and women know that this popular line of reasoning, through attractive, is not true. Real love is robust, strong, and resilient. It holds messy people together through almost unbearably tough times. The promise in the old cookbook is that "love never fails" (I Corinthians 13:8). Emotions, on the other hand, are flimsy and come and go with the wind. Love endures (more on this in Section III).

The idea that love is a matter of chance seems to be rooted in an ancient pagan fertility rite that celebrated adolescents' coming of age and the preparation for spring planting. The annual mid-February ceremony began in Rome 400 years before Christ's birth and lasted for another eight centuries.

In this primitive dating app utilized across the Roman Empire, young girls who were single and ready to mingle put their names in a basket. Then they gathered in the town square and stood by, anxiously pulling at their garments and checking their breath. Excitement built as the young boys of the city, one at a time, drew a girl's name from the basket. The "lucky" girl would then be assigned as the young man's mate, "to have and to hold" until the next February drawing. This mirrors our custom of drawing names at Christmas, with one significant difference. It really mattered who you were assigned to have and hold in ancient Rome.

Though the annual game of Love by Chance ended in 496 AD, one martyred saint remains synonymous with this love lottery notion 1,500 years later. His tragic love story began with his execution in 270 AD. By that time, Rome's powers and influence reached across Europe and into the Middle East. The Romans ruled from England in the north to Africa in the south and from Iran in the east to Spain in the west. The many wars necessary to sustain this kingdom required an endless supply of bodies to wield the empire's swords and shields. Eventually, that supply slowed down. As a result, the Roman legions were running out of able-bodied young men who were willing to leave their wives and families to fight, sometimes for years at a stretch. Under Roman rule, men with families could apply for exemption from military service, which left young, unattached boys and inexperienced young men as the only candidates for service.

If only there were a way to keep men from marrying, at least for a while. Then, there would be no marital exemptions, and the pool of potential legionnaires could increase significantly.

The solution came to the industrious Claudius II as if sent from above. Never one to be shy about his power, Claudius II essentially banned marriage by not allowing bishops to perform the ceremonial rites of marriage. Enter stage left: the Bishop of Interamna, also known as Reverend Valentine. Valentine lived and worked in Terni, about forty miles north of Rome. It was whispered that Valentine was the only bishop in the region willing to defy the Emperor's edict and perform potentially life-saving marriages. Of course, Claudius II got wind of this sedition and had Valentine arrested and jailed on suspicion of performing holy matrimony. While enduring torture and awaiting execution, Valentine struck up a relationship with his blind jailer's daughter. The relationship was short-lived but apparently passionate. Before entering the courtyard for his beheading, the amorous bishop left his new love a short note expressing his affection. It was signed, *From your Valentine*. The Catholic Church later bestowed sainthood on Valentine, and to this day we remember St. Valentine's Day with notes to lovers sometimes signed with the martyr's exact words.

Through the ages, the concept of love as a game of chance has endured and continues with the martyred St. Valentine perpetually overseeing the mid-February lottery. In Section III, I will have more to say about whether love comes by chance or choice. Spoiler alert: Although you'll have to ante up, true love is not a game of chance.

Chapter 6

THE ODDS FAVOR MARRIAGE

"Ye shall know the truth and the truth shall make you free."
—John 8:32 (NKJ)

THE OVERALL HEALTH OF A marital relationship, originally designed to last a lifetime, has been severely tested and questioned recently. More distressing is that some of the most negative reviews of marriage are given in, of all places, the modern church. Ironically, it is from the pulpit that you're most likely to hear statistics that extol today's sorry state of marriage. It is a rare minister that has not, with great gusto and regularity, referred to phantom statistics that predict half of the marriages performed this year will end in divorce, that infidelity is more likely than not, or—shamefully—most married people are unhappy. None of these statements are true.

As your social media feeds verify, there's plenty of work for divorce attorneys and therapists, but most of our marriages are okay, if not thriving. The numbers that the world's Eeyores refer to trace back to Shere Hite's sad statistics reported in the late 1980s. In 1987 Hite published *Women and Love: A Cultural Revolution in Progress*, a book that dug into the statistics produced by over 4,000 survey responses from readers of her earlier book, *The Hite Report: A Nationwide Study of Female Sexuality*.

Hite gave women a chance to vent with her first book, and they took her up on it. In her subsequent book, she minced few words in calling men out, labeling them (sometimes fairly) as domineering and condescending and worse. She reported that 89 percent of the married women in her response pool had unhappy marriages and that three quarters admitted to affairs. Any way you slice it, that's bad news. Like most bad news, it was reported widely and inaccurately, but her sad stories of love gone wrong had "legs," as TV executives say.

Luckily, there is some good news to report. Don't spread this around, but in towns and cities across America, there's a significantly high number of married people openly practicing monogamy. Hite's sad news is at best misleading and at worst, plain wrong. Her data were terribly biased. Remember, her survey sample primarily included her readership with a meager 4-percent return rate. Hite dutifully crunched these small numbers and reported them as proof that marriage is a failing institution. For the naysayers, it was delicious fodder for sensational headlines. But it remains lousy science.

The statistic that 50 percent of marriages end in divorce isn't much better. Sure, it's good arithmetic, but it's bad science. This percentage comes from data from the National Center for Health Statistics, an organization that tracks the number of marriages and divorces in a given year for *We the people.*[*] As you will see, over the past few years, the number of marriages has hovered around 2 million per year. In that same period, there was an annual average of approximately 0.8 million divorces. To a sixth grader handy with long division or an adult with a calculator, that works out to about one divorce for every two marriages each year or 40 percent, which evangelistically rounds up to 50 percent.

The numbers are right, but the conclusions are wrong. My happy marriage did not end this past year. To test the concept, take an informal and unscientific poll at your work or church. Count the marriages and divorces. I suspect the rate will not approach the 50-percent standard your preacher relays on Sunday morning.

---

* *Don't take my word for it. Check the stats for yourself.* *https://www.cdc.gov/nchs/fastats/marriage-divorce.htm*

The underreported good news is that 50 percent is way off. There are many factors to consider and ways to approach the question, but one simple and direct way to gauge the prevalence of divorce is to look at folks who are either married or widowed and ask about their experience with divorce. One reputable research center has done this on a large scale.

Since 1972, the University of Chicago's National Opinion Research Center (NORC) has operated on National Science Foundation grants to manage a variety of data about us. Their General Social Survey (GSS), conducted about every other year, draws from a random sample of Americans to reach generalizations about the American public with a high degree of confidence. Their scientific surveys cover a wide variety of topics, from our health to our habits. Their site (norc.org) is a treasure trove for curious minds. They invite you to use their data and will even help you learn how to best understand it.

Table 1, taken from GSS survey results, offers strong evidence that divorce is not as prevalent as most suspect. NORC repeatedly gathers responses to the question, If currently married or widowed: have you ever been divorced or legally separated? Focusing on five years of data on this straightforward question, it's easy to see that divorce does not impact half of the married people in our country. Over the years, about 75 percent of our friends and neighbors have never consulted a divorce attorney.

That's great news that should be spread with the same excitement as the media spreads Hite's sham science. However, the data also reveal an alarming rise in the percentage of married couples who dissolved their union. In 1972, only 14.5 percent of those surveyed experienced divorce. In the latest survey (2022), that percentage increased to 27.7 percent, representing more than a 90-percent increase. That may have to do with the sad tale regarding matrimony our children are hearing. Many of us are guilty of repeating the erroneous notion that half of all marriages end in divorce. I think that malicious gossip has dented the expectations of vulnerable marriage candidates, setting up expectations of failure. Literally, for goodness's sake, let's look on the brighter side. There is good news to tell.

On the question of marital happiness, there is yet more good news

Table 1. *1972-2022 Responses to Survey Question: If currently married or widowed: Have you ever been divorced or legally separated?*

	1972	1990	2000	2021	2022
Response did not apply or question skipped	352	478	1288	1732	1832
Yes	183 (14.5%)	194 (21.7%)	357 (23.3%)	605 (26.3%)	475 (27.7%)
No	1078 (85.5%)	700 (78.3%)	1172 (76.7%)	1695 (73.7%)	1237 (72.3%)
Total	1261	894	1529	2300	1712

for marriage buffs. Lucas, Clark, and Diener (2003) conducted a fifteen-year longitudinal study of life satisfaction in 24,000 adult subjects. They reported a connection between marital status and general happiness and a slight boost in the measures of life satisfaction from marriage. To no one's surprise, the rise in happiness levels seem linked to the increased social support, companionship, and shared experiences that come with most marriages. Though happiness levels during the adjustment phase in new marriages dip slightly, married couples consistently seem happier than their single peers. These findings echo an overwhelming number of studies that have—contrary to naysayers—consistently reported that most marriages (including mine and, I hope, yours) are happy.

It is generally whispered, even in polite circles, that most people cheat on their spouses. When pressed for evidence, almost everyone can name at least one person in their phone contacts who is slipping or has slipped around. However, hearsay was never good enough for *Dragnet's* Sargent Joe Friday. To prove the point, you need hard data, or as Sargent Friday deadpanned, "Just the facts, ma'am." When held to that standard, even this most threatening of marital difficulties wilts. Simply put, most people don't cheat. In another survey of readers, *Psychology Today* reported in 1992 that 90 percent of married couples have been faithful throughout their married lives. Interestingly, a vast majority (87 percent) believed they were more concerned with faithfulness than others.

Two years later, *Time* magazine asked 3,500 randomly selected Americans ages eighteen to fifty-nine similar questions for their October 17, 1994, Sex Survey Edition. They reported an astounding 94 percent of marriage partners were faithful to their spouses during the previous year. Their results further indicated that 85 percent of women and 75 percent of men had never been unfaithful. In a world that insists marital unfaithfulness is the standard, few couples realize their faithfulness makes them part of the norm.

In perhaps the best news of all, the *Washington Post* and *ABC News* reexamined Hite's juicy but suspicious bad news. They took her same questions and surveyed a larger, randomly selected sample, as science demands. Their results indicated that 93 percent were in happy marriages and only 7 percent ever engaged in an extramarital affair.

Table 2. *1973-2022 Responses to Survey Question: Taking things all together, how would you describe your marriage? Would you say your marriage is very happy, pretty happy, or not too happy?*

	1973	1990	2000	2021	2022
Response did not apply or question skipped	432	648	1553	2046	2089
Very happy	727 (67.8%)	468 (64.4%)	789 (62.4%)	1211 (61.0%)	881 (60.5%)
Pretty happy	317 (29.6%)	240 (33.1%)	434 (34.3%)	701 (35.3%)	502 (34.5%)
Not too happy	28 (2.6%)	16 (2.2%)	41 (3.2%)	74 (3.7%)	72 (4.9%)
Total	1072	724	1264	1986	1455

Condensed from five selected years of the General Social Survey (GSS) at the National Opinion Research Center (NORC) at the University of Chicago available at https:// gssdataexplorer.norc.org/variables/435/vshow

There are likely many alternative explanations for what Andrew Greeley called "a fidelity epidemic." Whatever the reason, the good news of marriage's excellent health needs to be told at least as often as we sound its death knell. The children in our congregations are bombarded with the perception that half of all marriages don't last, most couples are unhappy, and most spouses cheat. None of these statistics are true. Enter a covenant relationship with those beliefs, and the first signs of trouble will send the newlywed packing. Then, that couple becomes a member of that faceless and nameless crowd: *everyone*. You can reduce their risk. Correct them with the good news, provide concrete evidence that everybody's NOT doing it! Sargent Friday and countless spouses and children will thank you.

The sheer number of gossip publications, salacious TV shows, and social media traffic suggests a national, collective obsession with all things regarding human relationships. We may shrug them off, but such relationships matter. They matter because God is relational, and he designed us to be relational beings. In these relationships we practice our Sunday School lessons and try out those fancy Greek *love* verbs the pastor learned in Seminary. Crazily enough, unconditional love for another benefits the lover as much as the loved. Even the most cynical must admit the genius in this original design for messy humans. Maybe Tom Cruise was right. In a mysterious way, one incomplete human being almost completes another.

Bags of dirt are admittedly imperfect, and that description fits most of us. Consequently, the never-ending quest of finding the "perfect one" is a monumental waste of time that runs contrary to God's original plan. We choose a partner, then do what's necessary to make it work. However gloomy that sounds, for those committed to loving another without any strings attached, the odds are overwhelmingly in your favor. For candidates who are fully committed to the original design of marriage, I bet you'll stay married, your spouse will be faithful, and you'll be happy. Looking at the stats, you should take that bet as well.

As we will discover in the next two sections, this success is why men and women leave the comforts of the familiar and cleave to one another.

Section II

NOTES ON *LEAVING*: MARRIED LOVE'S FIRST PRIMARY INGREDIENT

At the still point of the turning world . . . there the dance is.
—T.S. Eliot from *Burnt Norton*

Overview

This section focuses on leaving, an often-misunderstood notion that is an odd prerequisite to cleaving. Leaving is the first of two biblical ingredients for homemade, married love and a healthy marriage, but unfortunately not a lot of fun to talk about. While *cleaving* conjures notions of loving and intimacy, *leaving* requires a farewell to parts of a life—old habits and former girlfriends or boyfriends that were important to your personal development. As if kissing all that goodbye were not difficult enough, leaving demands self-sacrifice, something most of us are not crazy about. Nonetheless, the sometimes-painful process of parting ways with single life is a necessary first step in becoming a successful cleaver. If you're not good at leaving, you will struggle with cleaving. Conversely, if you're having difficulty cleaving, you might want to take a hard look at your leaving strategies and make some adjustments.

Leaving in a marriage context informs the fateful question candidates are likely to be asked at the altar, "Will you forsake all others and cling only to this one?" Biblical leaving is certainly not permission to leave the other and abandon the marriage when the road gets rocky. It is the opposite. To hold tight to your partner in tough times, it's often necessary to let go of other people, things, and traditions that were former sources of comfort, bits and pieces that defined a life.

Together, couples forge ahead with the promises inherent in a bond not conditioned on health, wealth, or status. This level of commitment makes it easier to lay down those parts of life that get in the way. This mature version of love is reflected in John 15:13, "Greater love hath no man (or woman) than this, that he (or she) lay down his (or her) life for his (or her) friend" (paraphrased). Very rarely are men or women required to take a bullet for their spouse, but almost every day, love asks that lovers lay down pieces of their lives for their closest friend in the world. Marriage is a grownup, emotionally expensive proposition that begins with both partners leaving things that were once precious or comfortable. Such leaving is a sacrificial act that makes it possible to cleave to the beloved unencumbered.

Biblical leaving involves biology, sociology, and a healthy dose of theology. Its impact marks every facet of life. Each leaving situation is loaded with consequences that shape our lives and fortunes. Some of these significant episodes are conscious decisions to leave based in hard reality, such as a job change or going off to college. Other leaving decisions are made below the level of consciousness, deep in the DNA, or are the result of an unseen developmental schedule—e.g., a baby fighting to leave the warmth and safety of the womb for the outside world where alone, she stands no chance.

Scary as leaving may be, it's necessary. We can't remain the same and keep breathing. Staying in one place—literally and figuratively—is a sure-fire prescription for death. The heart is never still for too long on this side of the pearly gates. The only way to experience the wonders of being thirty years old is to leave the twenties, and if you have any interest in being my age, you must get comfortable with leaving a host of decades in the rearview mirror. Lean into leaving. It's a major part of living.

As the bathroom mirror and old family photos remind us, time changes us in profound ways. Tastes in fashion, how we talk, and what we thought was so neat, cool, or hip is the target of ridicule today. If we obeyed the familiar advice in high school annuals to never change, we would all dress in the preferred high school uniform of the gang we ran with in our teen years. Some of us were nerds or jocks, others were preppies, a few were skater dudes, and a sufficient number fell into my bunch, the rednecks. Like the cheerleaders and gangsters, we all got the memo on acceptable costume. A cheerleader could recognize other cheerleaders and wouldn't be caught dead dressed like a redneck. Each group had its own jargon and an unwritten code of behavior that we thought would last forever. Oh, we were wrong.

The world kept turning, and most of us got real jobs and we adapted. The alternative was unacceptable. If we stayed the same, we wouldn't grow intellectually, socially, or psychologically. For all of us, those "Glory Days" Bruce Springsteen sang of were powerful, but even "the Boss" reminded us we have to move on. Each of us must come to grips with what Bradley Cooper sang in a *A Star Is Born*, that the time will come when we must let the old ways die.

What I think you've figured out by now is that things change. That brief sentence explains aches and pains and the ravages of time. Everything we see, touch, smell, feel, and think is subject to change. The one exception: the still point around which the world revolves. Whether we like it or not, days, seasons, time, work, and feelings all change. High school reunions, our children, and the calendar on the wall are reminders that we change—our bodies, what we like or don't like, what we believe or don't believe. Eliot's "still point in the turning world" is the one constant that can anchor a life in a perpetual state of flux.

For me, that point is the Creator of all that is, the Alpha and the Omega, the beginning and the end. This God designed us individually, and as the creator of the first day, he is keenly aware of the ticking clock he set in motion and its impact on every aspect of our lives. What happens to his creation matters to him. As one writer put it, "He so loved the world" (John 3:16) he created.

I believe as God was putting our world together, he knew the end from the beginning. He understood the frailty inherent in his human creation and was aware of the limited ability of it to face the changing world without help. Early on, he said, "It is not good that man should be alone" (Genesis 2:18) and subsequently created someone to help Adam through life's inevitable ups and downs.

This first arranged marriage was built on the solid commitment to two fundamental obligations in marriage: leaving and cleaving. Leaving, the clear and stark prerequisite to cleaving, and all of its implications, rights, and privileges, is an uncomfortable proposition. However, it is the first obligation in a sound marriage. Turning your back on the way things *were* and casting your lot with your beloved in the way things *will be* is a sobering notion that makes cleaving work. It is the easily overlooked first responsibility of marriage partners that is intricately woven into the tapestry of life.

Leaving has unfortunately been maligned by our culture, in our poetry and paintings, Top 40 songs and podcasts, novels and movies. As a result, leaving is a largely forgotten part of the sacred marriage vow. The scary notion of turning away from the familiar to embrace an uncertain future is not for the weak hearted. Leaving demands courage and a strong faith in the future, both which are uncommonly rare and unpopular in our me-first world. But as Maya Angelou wrote, *All God's Children Need Traveling Shoes*.

In this section, I offer a brief examination of how leaving, the first piece of biblical advice on marriage and one of two primary ingredients in love making, is a natural function of the process of living and dying. The urge to leave seems to be profoundly rooted in the DNA of all living things and ultimately connected to the natural processes of growth and development.

While the *why* of leaving can be debated, it is agreed that leaving is the stuff of a solid foundation for a healthy marriage. In marriage, candidates must forsake all others, never look back, and build a new life with the beloved. These are difficult asks for human beings absorbed with their own importance. However, the payoff for those who yield to love's first demand is a rich life of willing sacrifice and amazing grace that undergirds this noble sacrifice of self. Leaving in this sense, even if truly for the good, still does not make it easy.

What I know best is my own struggle in leaving and the role tradition played in nurturing and discouraging this difficult first step toward maturity and loving. It's a personal story, and the only one I can write about with full permission. Along the way I've learned a lot about forsaking all others, and my hope is that my mistakes are learning opportunities that will improve your judgment. Mark Twain suggested, "Good judgment comes from experience and experience comes from bad judgment." If that's true, I've had a lot of experience.

CHAPTER 7

FIRST THINGS FIRST

Marvin K. Mooney, will you please go now?

—Dr. Seuss

LEAVING IS ONE OF TWO foundational requirements in a marriage and precedes the more widely known and celebrated cleaving. Leaving the known, comfortable, and established is a frightening first step of faith in building a new life with your beloved. There are few guarantees, but the choice to cut the strings that bind is consequential. Without discarding some of your former self, there can be no *us*, no butterflies on the summer milkweeds. My hope is that this section helps calm the jitters that "forsaking all others" tends to conjure and provoke a fresh appreciation for the intelligent design woven into the DNA of God's cute but cantankerous, imperfect children. No matter how we understand the rationale, leaving is at the top of the to-do list for the ragged, imperfect souls at the marriage altar. We might as well embrace this necessary first step toward connubial bliss. After all, each of us, including Marvin K. Mooney, must eventually leave.

Tangled up in leaving is a complicated knot of feelings that range from palpable fear, hints of apprehension, and a tinge of excitement. Moms and dads who send children to college, into the military, or across town know that goodbyes, however temporary, are emotional and potentially life-changing events. From the day a child enters a family's life, the parents know this day of leaving is inevitable. Down deep they know their task as parents is to work themselves out of a job, to necessarily become unnecessary. Effective parents train their babies to make it on their own. It is their responsibility to provide the kid in the Honda the necessary tools to survive and thrive in the big world at the end of the driveway. For the kid, the excitement of new places and possibilities is mingled with some apprehension and lots of internal questions. *Am I ready for this? What happens if I can't measure up? How much of myself will I give? How do I do laundry?*

The kid's feelings and questions are common. To those at the matrimonial altar, the questions are oddly familiar. In a real sense, the marriage candidates are leaving home, which is either a place where they have been cared for, protected, and sheltered by adults or a home they personally carved out of a rock-hard world in which they found safety. Leaving the comforts of home, as teens and fiancés know, is a scary and difficult proposition, but is as necessary as a three-year-old black bear cub wandering off in the woods to scratch out a life of his own. Failure to launch infects about one-third of all young adults who are either unprepared or not ready to leave home. They simply can't seem to create the secure environment or comfort levels that mirror those found at their parents' place. Returning home, or boomeranging, is often the path of least resistance. Yes, leaving is the first step in taking charge of a life and enjoying the rights and privileges of the most prized possession any of us will ever have, the self. It is also a frightening proposition. Chicks who never leave the warmth and safety of the shell or young adults who can't get out of Mom's basement don't make it. It sounds harsh, but it's reality.

The necessity of leaving the comforts of home is not about distance. Married men and women who move across the country can remain bound by Mom's apron strings. These folks have trouble choosing a bathroom paint color without consulting their parents. What they don't realize is that the person whose opinion matters more is on the other side of the bed. On the other hand, some move into their parents' neighborhood and maintain a healthy level of independence.

The big ask at the altar is to take that first step of trading familiar

Saturday morning routines, eating habits, and ways of doing laundry for an uncertain future and promises of love. That giant leap requires resilience and raw faith in the power of love to transform two individuals into one, without losing either personality. The foundation of that kind of confidence is dug out of the dirt in childhood and in ordinary events that take on significance only in the past tense. The deep roots of current conflicts and differences in a marriage are often traceable to events that happened long ago.

CHAPTER 8

WHY WE LEAVE

A foolish consistency is the hobgoblin of little minds.
—Ralph Waldo Emerson

NOT MANY OF US ARE unmoved by cute kittens at the local pound. Their wide-set eyes are bright, their colorful coats are shiny, and their bodies are full of energy. It's easy to imagine their playfulness lighting up an empty apartment or entertaining the kids, and—best of all—they don't need batteries. Give them a place to sleep and keep them fed and watered and everything will be just peachy . . . at least for a while. The issue is that kittens tend to outgrow that friendly, selfless, carefree attitude a few days after you get them home. As Ogden Nash noted, "The trouble with a kitten is that eventually it becomes a cat."

We shouldn't be surprised. Like us, cats' attitudes change over time. A cat's tolerance for the crazy stuff in life tends to relate inversely to their age. You pet an old cat on the cat's terms, and as cats age, they get more like Garfield than Flopsy. Our old cat used to look at us as if to say, "You wanna play? Get a kid and go outside. This house is mine." Unfortunately, old cats sound a lot like old humans. I didn't mean to lose my playfulness or energy, but get off my lawn!

Speaking of leaving . . .

Leaving is in our nature. Put simply, living things leave. Living things grow, and growing is a long, slow process that involves leaving the old in favor of the new. Leaving is part of life. A newborn calf, ant larvae, and a caterpillar pupa must eventually leave comfortable surroundings for the unfamiliar. Despite what a twelve-year-old sixth grader thinks, change is coming. Given time, that twelve-year-old will turn thirteen, then in 365 days, he will reach fourteen. And if he continues to breathe, he soon will be eligible for a learner's permit and eventually have opportunity to graduate high school.

Navigating these constant changes are parents, who also constantly change, adapt, and learn. They have only 365 days to try parenting a twelve-year-old and figure out the dynamic of how the family fits together during that stage. Often, parents do so with little to no experience and a lot of frustration. About the time they learn the ropes, everything changes. They suddenly have to parent a thirteen-year-old.

We get only one shot, 365 days to be exact, at being a ten-year-old. By the time we get settled in, it's time to move on to the next year. We are constantly moving from one year to the next. That same process—passing between stages of life—happens over and over again, whether you agree or disagree with the changes at each stage. To survive, we mortals must move on and accept and deal with the changes at each stage.

Leaving Is Necessary in Living

Moving on with life requires us to leave. You can't get into double digit birthdays until you leave the single digits. Likewise, there's no fortieth birthday until the thirties get left behind. Every second we are alive involves leaving the previous second and what happened in it. The "way it used to be" is just that—a pile of old seconds we now call history. Conscious survivors of yesterday learn what works and what doesn't, what to avoid and what to embrace, information that shapes life in the coming seconds. Whether we like it or not, are prepared or unprepared, willing or unwilling, the next second is on its way and just behind it, another. As Chaucer wrote over 750 years ago, "time and tide wait for no man." Ironically, until you get comfortable with life's clock constantly running and the necessity of leaving a lot of stuff behind, it's difficult to really live. Embracing time and its ravages on everything except what T.S. Eliot called "the still point in the tunning world" forces you to get comfortable leaving things behind, a point accepted without contention by lower forms of life.

Like Eliot's cats—and all other living things—we're on a preprogrammed treadmill that goes from one mode to the next, often without warning. We can be cruising along at a soft comfortable pace and suddenly things change. Careless cats wander into the street for the last time. Young boys discover girls don't in fact have cooties. Loved ones get sick. The perfect job opens in another state. A lonely, sick young man thinks he can settle made-up grievances with a long gun. Comfortable, ordinary worlds fall apart in the wake of these unplanned abrupt disruptions in established routines. They force us to leave what we know and learn different skills if we are to survive. Despite what my first real girlfriend wrote in my high school annual, no one stays the same. Life is a series of events that forces us to settle in and then leave the comfort of our nests for the unfamiliar surroundings where we will either learn new coping skills or die. That pattern of self-discovery seems to be preprogrammed into our DNA. While most of these changes are beyond our ability to control, our reaction to them is not. Adaptation, then, is the secret superpower of long-lived things.

Life continues regardless of objections from old cats, young walruses, or middle-aged housewives. Its rhythm was set in motion long ago and remains beyond our ability to effectively alter. As aging starlets and athletes know too well, time is relentless. No amount of face cream or bench-pressing can stop time's relentless demands. As life evolves, voices, shoe sizes, skin elasticity, and more change. Eventually, the old guy who gets off life's treadmill is different from the small mass of protoplasm plopped on it years ago. Although we can sometimes control the speed, angle, and resistance of the treadmill, we cannot stop it without unplugging the machine.

As I've pointed out, leaving one set of circumstances for another is sometimes a conscious decision, but very often the change comes as a surprise. You can decide to leave a job, change schools, move to a new home, and update your relationship status. However, there are important leaving times preprogrammed in your genetic coding that shape you and bend the arc of your character. You don't decide to leave childhood or develop a life-threatening illness, but moving on with life demands that you stare down reality and pack your bags for a new destination.

At each of these inflection points there are consequential learning opportunities that impact development. Sooner or later, each of us will use up all chances to improve our leaving, with—if you will forgive me the poor pun—grave consequences. How we leave on that day matters. According to the World Population Review, about 8,000 Americans die every day. Like their peers who are accepting jobs, moving, or changing the status of their relationships, roughly ten Americans die every second for varied reasons. Some deaths are the sad result of bad choices, while others are mysterious and uncalled for. We have all attended enough funerals to know at the gut level that leaving is part of the bargain in living. Out of necessity, we make an uneasy peace with leaving. One way to soothe the paralyzing fear in leaving is to better understand and embrace its inevitability and what it teaches.

Living things must learn to be good leavers.

A Leaving Lesson from the Caterpillar

The caterpillar is a slow, deliberate, homely little creature with close-set, beady eyes and a hard face that only a mother could love. *Beautiful* is not the adjective of choice to describe this worm. However, as has been said about many of us, God's not done with the caterpillar . . . yet. To realize his potential, the caterpillar (like the rest of us) has some serious leaving to do. He spends the first part of his life crawling around on leaves, enjoying the all-you-can-eat buffet of a healthy tree. Then one day, a faint impulse pushes him to leave this idyllic life and for some crazy reason weave a silky blanket, hang it from a tree limb, and wrap up in it—*upside down*. To the old worm, this elaborate plan probably makes no sense. It doesn't have to. The caterpillar didn't design it, but he fully and completely trusts the mystery of his instinct.

I suspect that even hanging upside down, the mummified caterpillar and his pals catch fleeting glimpses of the breathtaking insects flying in and out of the tree's shadows. As they watch, it could never occur that these gorgeous critters were their cousins. No caterpillar wrapped in a comfortable cocoon dreams of soaring on summer breezes, flitting around flowers, and nibbling at the sweetest nectar available, all while wearing designer wings that would make Dolly Parton blush.

Like the caterpillar wrapped in a cozy, comfortable silk blanket, we have no way of knowing the essence and majesty of John's prophetic words: "it doth not yet appear what we shall be" (I John 3:2). Like the caterpillar, we won't fully know until we leave our present comforts for the promise "shut up in our bones" (Jeremiah, 20:9).

Living things must leave.

The Promise of a Second Chance

America is the story of brave pioneers who left comfort for promises of a better, but uncertain future "out there." They understood their current situations and felt things could be better, that life had more to offer. Sadly, not all of those with that nagging wanderlust survived, but those who did had a chance at a much brighter future. Unlike the butterfly, we continue repeating these brave pioneers' inspiring stories to this day.

The metamorphosis of the butterfly unfolds as a design of nature. Butterflies don't (or can't) decide to build a cocoon. They just do it. However, humans may have an unexplainable hankering to strike out in a new direction. When faced with such a desire, we can subject that urge to reasoned thought. We can decide where, when, how, and if we build a house. Successful pioneers in exploration, science, art, and relationships had an inkling, a curious wondering that does not occur to cocooned worms. Advances in human endeavor occur—as some have said— because we stand on the shoulders of giants. What we learn through often painful, personal, learned experiences is that we need each other, as our chances of success in business and other realms improves when we partner up.

The stresses and strains of modern living are difficult to bear alone. We need reassurance that someone has our back. When we are quiet and not distracted by modern conveniences and responsibilities, we're more likely to tell ourselves this unvarnished truth. What generally emerges from those late-night individual therapy sessions is the fact that each of us is limited, a brutal truth that's hard to face in the daylight. As surely as I can help you design a reasonably reliable survey instrument, I am absolutely no help in fixing your car or balancing a checkbook. Consequently, I have a host of painful stories spotlighting my weaknesses and inabilities. Praise God, I married well!

The choice of my wife as a marriage partner fifty-three years ago offered me a chance to start over. A new branch in our family tree budded that day in August of 1971. Jodi accepted me as a marriage partner knowing full well that I was pretty good at some things and terrible at others. She knew me in the dark moments and in the daylight, and despite this intimate knowledge, she promised before God and witnesses to love me faithfully, whatever happened. Over the years, our branch on the family tree, nourished with honest and abiding love, has grown stronger and more resilient, and its off shoots have flourished. Our adventures have enriched our lives and—I hope—inspired our children to trust in the power and promises found in loving one another.

CHAPTER 9

"THAT'S NOT HOW I WAS RAISED": A PERSONAL LEAVING STORY

"Whither thou goest, I will go; and where thou lodgest, I will lodge: thy people shall be my people . . ."

—Ruth 1:16

WHEN I ASKED JODI TO marry me, we had little in common. Our success as a married couple hinged on our willingness to adapt to new and unfamiliar traditions, customs, ways of talking, and circles of friends. Leaving is strenuous work, and the pasture I called Jodi to was not greener than the upper-middle-class home of her youth. Her decision to leave probably didn't make sense to her dad. Frankly, I was embarrassed to ask her to do it. Thank God, I did ask, and she accepted. So, we left, hand in hand.

I was raised in a strict Christian home south Georgia. Throughout my childhood, my parents had me and my four siblings in church every time the doors were open. Preachers constantly warned against the evils of smoking and drinking and hanging out in places where those "mortal sins" were likely practiced. There were lots of places on the Don't Let Me Catch You There list: bowling alleys, professional baseball games, and movie theaters, especially Sunset Drive-In. After all, what if God came back and caught you with a bowling ball stuck to your thumb? The exhaustive and ever-growing list of dos and don'ts were part of my cultural upbringing that got hammered into all Riggins children in a resource-poor, love-rich environment.

Growing Up

The seven of us lived in a series of shotgun houses around a sawmill in Dock Junction. Daddy worked at the sawmill Monday through Friday, and to make ends almost meet, he cut hair on the weekends. With no formal education in the barbering arts, his side hustle was driven by the hunger of six dependents. We hit the big-time when the aging sawmill owner sold Daddy a $200 piece of land on which we built a small six-room house. I was in fourth grade at the time. My family was so proud, but no one's pride outdid mine.

Nine years later, I was ready to take on the world. Like my buddies and brothers, I was young and inexperienced, eager to get out on my own. I had just graduated from high school, and as Daddy bragged at the annual family reunion, I did something unique. "He ain't even flunked a grade," Daddy said. My chest puffed out every time. But I couldn't afford to flunk any grades. I had big plans. Seaboard Construction Company, where I worked most summers, promised me a truck to drive and a raise to $1.35 an hour. With that kind of money, I could see the inside of the Brunswick Bowlarena and even drive a hot date through the front entrance of the Sunset Drive-In one Friday night. Like Travis Tritt, I was ten feet tall and bulletproof. I drove too fast, swam in sketchy creeks and rivers, and dated girls that offended Mama's tender sensibilities. Though I didn't recognize it at the time, my automobile insurance rate was a clear indicator of my immaturity and wanton willingness to take chances and assume risks for which I was woefully unprepared. But I could talk a good game.

What I Learned in College

In August of 1965, my post-high school plans stalled out. Seaboard Construction Company reneged on my truck and the ten-cent raise, and I got hot. One Friday afternoon, my friend Warren Mann suggested we enroll at Brunswick Junior College. There was just one problem. Monday was the last day to register. I didn't know a single college graduate and only knew one person who ever tried (that was my smart cousin Carolyn), but Warren promised to show me the ropes. That Friday afternoon, I turned in my Seaboard Construction Company shovel—the only thing they let me drive—and left.

Monday morning, Warren and I headed to Brunswick Junior College. Soon, I was assigned an advisor, the kindhearted English professor Dr. Betty Jo Strickland. After talking a bit, she handed me an overwhelming document with column after column of classes and days and meeting times. She then handed me a single sheet of paper, which she called a "trial schedule." Six rows ran across the top, listing hours of the day from 8 a.m. to 4 p.m., and the days of the week were listed in columns on the left. Dr. Strickland, who I later worked for as a student assistant, told me to pick out my classes, write my selections in the blank spaces on the trial schedule, and bring my completed paper back the next day. I was overwhelmed. I was also too embarrassed to admit it, so I backed out of her office and drove home.

That night, my brothers and sisters and Mama gathered around the table to help me fill out my trial schedule. I felt like the golden child, secretly loving when my brothers called me College Boy. My admission to college was about more than me. It was a family thing, and we had to get it right. As we filled in the blanks on my schedule, we ran into conflicts. One brother would suggest a class at a certain time, which conflicted with lab times. A sister would make another suggestion, but it met on the day of a required PE class. After at least three hours of trying to fit in all the classes I needed (or thought I needed), we gave up, and I just filled in the blanks at random.

The next day, I was almost at the point of tears when I told Dr. Strickland of our struggles. My college career was going be sidelined by clerical errors before it ever started. Dr. Strickland gave me a compassionate look and said, "Let me see if I can help." She took my trial schedule with its crossed-out classes and gummed-up erasure marks. Her wry smile and choked chuckle did not help my wounded pride. She said that the college operated in the quarter system, so I only had to take three or four classes. "What?" I asked. I thought college was like high school, only harder. I assumed, as Daddy said, college "Took in at eight and let out at five." Otherwise, why have all of those blank spaces? Consequently, I had a class in every hour of every day during the week. That was my uncomfortable introduction to higher education. I quickly adjusted. I even played on the college baseball team and met some wonderful friends who were much more sophisticated than me.

After two years, I left home for Georgia Southern University three hours away. Daddy came for one last hug in the driveway before I left. After looking around to make sure no one was watching, he got out his billfold, thumbed through it, and found a five-dollar bill. He crammed his such-as-I-have gift in my pocket, and without looking at me, said "Keep it." That five dollars was one of the most precious gifts I've ever received.

At the university my dorm room wasn't as cramped as the bedroom I shared with my two brothers, but it was beyond Mama's line of sight. To this naïve, first-generation college kid, everything was new, and—at first—exciting. I didn't know any students and seemed to have little in common with them. Kids openly smoked and drank and girls used more cuss words than I knew existed. I felt like I showed up at the formal wearing just flip-flops and undies. I finally understood the lyrics of the song we so often sang in church: "I am a pilgrim and a stranger, traveling through this wearisome land."

In classes, I was challenged by the ancient classics to expand my thinking in ways I never considered. One professor's final exam consisted of a single question he wrote on the board the first day of class, What is the good life? My task was to submit a paper the last day that explained my personal opinion on that fundamental question after considering a variety of views from the class's impressive assigned reading list. That forced me, for perhaps the first time, to examine what I thought and anchor it to something more solid that my limited opinion or what I'd heard while growing up.

I struggled through each text, but I was drawn to Herman Hess's *Siddhartha*, Orwell's *1984*, and Shakespeare's plays. I read Hamlet in high school, but I read it again with a renewed interest and fresh perspective. In the first act, Polonius's son Laertes is leaving for France, so Polonius offers his boy some traveling advice. He said,

> . . . these few precepts in thy memory . . . Be thou familiar, but by no means vulgar. / Those friends thou hast, and their adoption tried, / Grapple them to thy soul with hoops of steel; / But do not dull thy palm with entertainment / Of each new-hatched, unfledged comrade. / Beware of entrance to a quarrel . . . Give every man thy ear, but few thy voice; / Take each man's censure, but reserve thy judgment . . . the apparel oft proclaims the man . . . /Neither a borrower nor a lender be; / For the loan oft loses both itself and the lender, / And borrowing dulls the edge of husbandry. / This above all: to thine ownself be true, / And it must follow, as the night the day, / Thou canst not then be false to any man. / Farewell: my blessing season this in thee!
>
> —Act I, Scene iii

I couldn't believe it! This sounded like something my own daddy would have said, though with a lot more flair and a touch of poetic eloquence. Though the sentiment was about the same, the words giving them wings were a foreign language in Dock Junction. My pop's third grade education clearly limited his vocabulary, but not his ability to get his message across. Like Polonius, my daddy loved his boy, and his boy knew it. Daddy told me as much several times without fancy nouns and verbs. He taught master classes in respecting others, working hard, shouldering responsibility, and being satisfied with the best you can do. I like to think Leo Rosten (1986) had Daddy in mind when he wrote, "It is the weak who are cruel. Gentleness comes only from the strong."

As children of the bitter Depression that ravaged our nation and robbed families of hopes and dreams, my parents were well acquainted with circumstances beyond an individual's control. Accordingly, they prepared their kids for a world that would challenge them and could turn hostile without warning. That's the backdrop for my daddy's favorite piece of advice when I asked complicated gray-area questions. Taking his time, Daddy would push up his glasses with a bent first finger, smile, and say, "Son, you gotta learn to butt with your own head." As I later learned in an upper division literature class, Daddy's sage advice reflected Mark Twain's great line probably aimed at one of his girls. Twain stated, "If you pick up a cat by its tail, you'll learn things you cannot learn any other way."

Like Daddy, Twain knew the hard truth that no matter how loved they may be, children eventually leave home to make their way in a world that punches back. In one form or another, parental instruction boils down to helping children get ready spiritually, psychologically, behaviorally, and emotionally to leave home. Though they rarely talk about it, moms and dads and their babies know this day is inevitable. Bear parents instinctively know that if that learning is to be effective, the kid has to be personally involved. Nature and employers are unforgiving.

Resilience is one of the best indicators of a child's readiness for leaving. In fact, the gift of grit may be the most prized inheritance a child is bequeathed. Although the word resilience was never in my pop's vocabulary, he knew resilience and taught it by example. He was sure that without firsthand trial-and-error learning, it's difficult to build up enough callouses on the ego to survive.

In simple ways, Daddy let each of his children figure things out in our own way. Of course, we found the boundaries several times and trespassed on occasion. His go-to advice to "Do the right thing" seemed simplistic at the time, but it kept us between the ditches. Later, I learned that doing the right thing is a lot more important than doing things right. Rules for how things should be done change, but the fundamental why is consistently constant. Daddy knew that down deep, where words don't fit feelings.

Daddy's simple advice traveled well and covered almost every situation from hauling cows to shining shoes. It helped me solve little problems, but the size of problems seemed to grow as I did. At eight, I started shining shoes at the barber shop where daddy was learning to cut hair. I messed up a bunch of old men's shoes and endured ridicule from school friends, but at the end of a long Saturday, I had change rattling around in my pocket. The next day, I could chip in on the Sunday morning tithe and have enough left over for a Coke and candy bar at Aspinwall's grocery after church. It didn't occur to me at the time, but Daddy's guidance was helping me acquire that fundamental word he couldn't define or spell—resilience.

When my first semester from home was ending and my paper on The Good Life was taking shape, I reevaluated the people, circumstances, and events that formed the kid sitting at the library desk late at night reflecting on his Good Life. Moved to tears, I wrote my folks a long love letter full of gratitude and apologies. An old quote attributed to Mark Twain is good evidence that my development stages were not so unique. He—or someone else, perhaps—wrote, "When I was a boy of fourteen, my father was so ignorant I could hardly stand to have the old man around. But when I turned twenty-one, I was astonished at how much the old man had learned in just seven years." I guess I was a smidge faster than Twain. It only took a year away from my old man's favor to realize how I missed the security blanket of home. After four years of reading and considering a lot of great ideas and a few stupid ones, my university experience taught me that my version of The Good Life—sharing cramped spaces with my family and having a seat at Mama's all-you-can-eat buffet, was pretty sweet. When I graduated, I couldn't wait to get back to Dock Junction. Everything I loved was there. I wouldn't leave it again. I couldn't. It was home, and as we all know, home is where the heart is.

Two years later, I met Jodi.

The Comfortable Trap

Teachers and parents and bosses and bus drivers know it's hard to get anything done in chaotic situations. Very little is accomplished in the classroom, home, or workplace until order is restored. We need order to identify boundaries and clues about how to regulate our impulses and behavior so we learn to be productive members of our classes, families, and societies. The best and most effective early learning institution is the family.

Out of sheer necessity, families organize chaos into established routines that become ordinary, comfortable, and sometimes, sacred. Deciding not to enforce bedtime for early elementary kids is a way of ordering the chaos just as is setting a no-exceptions bedtime. Both are effective teaching mechanisms that yield very different outcomes.

It's surprisingly easy to settle into strange eating schedules, to go "nose blind" to funky smells, to fall into acceptable language patterns of a community, and to comply with laundry-sorting rituals. In some households, these mundane habits are treated as if stamped with the Good Housekeeping Seal of Approval by God. From there it's an easy jump to insist your way is the best way and everyone else does it wrong. Getting trapped in such conditioned comfort stymies our growth. We don't collect $200 dollars and never get past GO.

If or how you make your bed in the morning was probably established early in your life. The tradition is often as comfortable as your worn-out old couch and equally as hard to escape. However, love demands we leave home and its comfortable customs and cleave to one with a new set of opinions and expectations regarding bed-making and laundry. I can testify that this is not an easy ask, but as Scripture reminds us, it's one full of promise and blessing. Besides, this melding of two people into one offers a fresh start, a chance to reorder the chaos, another shot at redemption.

The One I Left For

In August of 1970, I saw her for the first time. I was standing outside the Chattanooga convention hall where our church was holding its annual international meetings when she walked through the double doors with her family. Her dad, a retired Air Force officer from South Dakota, came from a prominent family in our brand of Pentecostal churches, so his daughter was religious royalty to me. Appropriately, Jodi wore a purple dress and brushed her long blonde hair as she swept by. She glanced at me and, to her credit, hardly noticed my mouth gaping open like an eight-pound bass gasping for air. I was smitten, and she was clearly out of my league. Her family members were professionals. In addition to their many church heavyweights, Jodi's family included doctors, business owners, and her dad, a decorated flying officer in the Strategic Air Command. My family paled in comparison—barbers, farmers, truck drivers, welders, and my favorite uncle who worked his way up the sawmill's chain of command despite his inability to read.

At the time, Jodi attended a small church college in Cleveland, Tennessee, at her dad's insistence. ("Honey," he told her, "you can go anywhere, but I'll only pay tuition at this institution.") A classically trained pianist, Jodi was asked to play for the college's chorale, a small ensemble of students that toured churches on the weekends. As it just so happened ("Coincidences are God's way of remaining anonymous," as Buechner stated), the small church where my family found religion was on the chorale's 1970 New Year's itinerary.

I'd graduated college a year earlier and moved back into my old bedroom. I was in my second year of teaching curious seventh-graders about the complex behavior of atoms. In class we talked about how scientists broke down the building blocks of everything we taste, touch, and smell, but the really interesting part was the mystery of how electrons were attracted to each other. Our textbook described how mysterious magnetic forces were the most reasonable explanation for why some electrons paired up and others insisted on being alone. Notoriously, these tiny specks of nature didn't behave as Einstein's elegant theory of relativity predicted, but neither did I. I've since made peace with unexplainable behavior found in all kinds of relationships, especially between two humans.

In the first days of 1971, I knew something of words and language, but forgot it all when I rounded a corner in the church and literally ran smack into Jodi. She was quite simply the most beautiful collection of electrons I'd ever seen up close. I immediately detected evidence of that mysterious, magnetic universal force that often impairs speech and thought in humans. I somehow managed to get out an awkward "Hey!"

and pushed a few more syllables past the knot in my throat. She smiled and nodded, so I suppose some of my noises were intelligible. As the pianist for the chorale, Jodi was in a hurry. We agreed to talk more after church.

The singing that night was okay, but the piano playing was heavenly! Neither Mama, our regular piano player, nor Aunt Virgie ever played that piano with such grace and beauty, especially the latter. After the service, members of the group were assigned to lodge at homes of various congregation members. To echo Buechner, I won the lottery. Jodi and her friend were assigned to my house. My brother and I took the two girls out to eat after the concert, and Jodi and I sat up talking almost all night. Despite our differences in social rank, we had many similarities, and she was as easy to talk with as she was to look at. If I was smitten before, the evening left me gobsmacked.

School started back for me, so I had to go back to teaching about electrons. But Jodi's new semester wouldn't start for another week, so she and her friend, Sandra, drove back down to South Georgia the following weekend. Mama quietly panicked, unsure she had the resources or energy reserve to feed two guests all weekend long.

When Jodi and Sandra pulled up in Jodi's MGB convertible late Friday night, my whole family was on the front porch to greet them. As soon as they walked in, Daddy put Mama to work. "Jo," he said, "go fix these young 'uns sumpn' t' eat." Mama, ever prepared, hoped hot dogs would satisfy, and put sixteen of them in a pot to boil while the rest of us set the table for our two late-night diners. All the while, the girls demurred politely, insisting, "We're not hungry." It had an unintended effect. The more they protested, the more food Mama piled on the table.

After the dogs boiled sufficiently to do no harm, we got those two fancy college girls to our big table to enjoy some late-night hot dogs with all the fixin's. They weren't as hungry as we were curious. After we wore out the obvious small talk topics—the warm January weather in South Georgia and the rigors of an eight-hour drive, my daddy took the conversation in an unexpected direction. Never shy about talking to anyone about anything, he saw that neither girl had sampled Mama's hot weenies. Apparently, Daddy decided the girls needed a culinary lesson on the finer points of fixing a good hot dog. This kind and gentle soul reached over, pinched one of the fattest, most deformed weenies in the pot and waved it as a sort of visual aid. "Girls," he said, "this is how to cook a weeny. You gotta boil 'em till they bustes."

The girls took the lesson with what appeared to be sincere interest. That said, I'm pretty sure my daddy's simple, honest observation on preparing a good weenie was never discussed around the Colonel's table; however, it broke the ice that night as we laughed over our differences in hot dogs specifically, and how we were raised in general. Unknowingly, Daddy led a graduate lesson around that table on what great thinkers are still testing in high-tech laboratories. Maybe the mystery attraction that unites us—the rich and poor, the sophisticated and the uncultured, the old and young—is the longing to strip away the artificial differences in the trappings of our stations in life and tell our own truth. The petty differences that divide us, from how hot dogs ought to be prepared to how and where we worship, are just that—petty. But as divorce attorneys know, if these differences go ignored and get stuffed down, they rot. Place those differences on the table and talk about them with an honest sincerity and big dollop of laughter, and we can learn to boil weenies a little longer . . . or not.

Recently, scientists verified what Solomon hypothesized a few centuries back, "Laughter doeth good like a medicine" (Proverbs 17:22). A couple of millennia after Solomon prescribed this miracle cure, there is evidence that it works. Teresa Corrigan, an instructor at The University of California at San Francisco's Osher Center for Integrative Medicine, wrote "Not only does laughter boost our serotonin, dopamine, and endorphin levels . . . [but also] it is a great workout for the immune, lymph, and cardiovascular systems" (Craig, 2012, n.p.). Laughter and its sidekick, Happiness, may be what's missing in marriages that don't work. Several reliable studies (e.g., Pelzman, 2024; Rothwell, 2024; Smith, 1979) have reported significant associations between marriage and overall happiness, especially when compared with single peers. For those who may still doubt the connection between marriage and happiness in the general population, I invite you to search the gold-standard database for social research in America, the National Opinion Research Center (NORC) at the University of Chicago (https://www.norc.org/research/projects/gss.html). Based on the sheer volume of evidence it seems reasonable that married folks should expect happiness. So relax. Hug your sweetie and laugh a little. It will do you good.

A New Way to Fold Towels

One of the payoffs of leaving is the chance to learn new things, trade in old habits for new ones, and possibly enjoy a better life. Unfortunately, leaving and learning show up in work clothes. You have to do something, and some of your efforts will be at least slightly uncomfortable. However, there is a lot of black-and-white evidence in your family's old photograph albums that it's a risk worth taking.

By the middle of the 1960s, Daddy's barbering business was going strong. In a giant leap of faith, he left the sawmill and rented some space next to Mr. Brower's Grocery in Dock Junction to open his own shop. In short order, he traded his sawmill truck for a school bus. He used the bus to haul kids to and from school in the early morning and midafternoon, traditionally slow times in the barbering business.

Daddy wasn't the only one who worked. To keep our growing family of three sons, two daughters, and Mama and Daddy functioning, we had to master division of labor. While Daddy worked his two jobs, Mama and my sisters cooked three meals a day and did the laundry. The boys took care of the outside jobs—tending to the big garden and the livestock that fed us and the constant repairs on our farmhouse. On the weekends, we three boys shared the thriving shoeshine business at the barbershop and brought home money for groceries. We went to school about as often as we went to church. It was such a comfortable existence, and I thought it was the standard family model across the board. I was wrong.

Ironically, my dad's impromptu lesson on weenie cooking turned out to be a quirk that attracted Jodi. She loved Daddy's ability to be truly and wholly himself, at ease in every situation. Though he never read Walt Whitman, he personified the bard's line in *Leaves of Grass*, "In all men I see myself, none more and not one a single barley-corn less."

Jodi's surprising attraction to me and my family led her back to South Georgia several times after we met during the chorale's January tour. For some reason (aside from the culinary tips), she always stayed for Sunday dinner. Like the Masters Tournament, it was "a tradition like no other." Routinely, Mama and my sisters got up early Sunday morning to cut up and fry five chickens before we left for Sunday school. After some good hard preaching, they'd come home to whip up a big pot of rice and gravy, put two pans of biscuits in the oven, and make a gallon or two of sweet tea. Then my sisters would set the table with mostly matching plates and an almost full set of mason jars full of ice and ready for tea. After the blessing, it was a free-for-all.

Even after Mama's hard work was done, she never joined us at the table. She would fix her plate and sit in a chair between the kitchen and dining room, tending to the needs of her family or company. I never heard Dad ask Mama to get him some more tea. He simply held up his empty jar and rattled the ice without missing a beat in his story of the day. Mama or one of my sisters would then jump up and refill his glass. After Jodi and I married, I realized Jodi hadn't gone to the same finishing school as Mama. The first clue was that she sat at the table with me as we ate. I quickly learned that rattling ice in an empty glass was not the universal signal for someone to bring more tea. To her credit, Jodi was not scared off. My hunch is that the officers on the Air Force bases where Jodi grew up did things differently. It took some time, but I learned in our first year of marriage that tradition is a powerful teacher that's not always right. Jodi, a powerful teacher in her own right, helped me understand that in very real, practical ways.

Another hard piece of learning for me involved laundry. Other than throwing dirty clothes in a hamper, I had no experience with cleaning clothes. I had no clue what happened between the hamper and the fresh clothes in the tiny closet I shared with my brothers. Somehow, I picked up the notion that laundry was an inside chore and therefore off-limits for men. In my mind, there was a secret about mixing bleach and detergent that only women understood. And while men did not participate in indoor chores, they were free to opine on any inside chores not up to family standards. Or so I thought. Boy, was I wrong.

Not long after we married, Jodi graciously gave me a few rather emotional lessons on sorting and folding laundry. I learned that sorting dirty clothes into piles of different colors makes a difference. Previous to this lesson, I naively thought dirty clothes were dirty clothes. With this natural bent toward inclusion, I once mixed the whole rainbow into a single laundry cycle. After a long, tearful lecture on ruining clothes, Jodi gave a quick tutorial on sorting. We settled the issue and as a bonus, I got a set of tie-dyed underwear that Jimi Hendrix would have been proud of. Inspired by her student's attentiveness, Jodi finished the series of lectures by teaching me what to do with clothes after they were cleaned and dried.

In college, the method I used to pack clothes for Mama and my sisters to wash resembled Lucille Ball's technique for stuffing chocolate boxes on an assembly line. I crammed a lot in college, and sometimes I even studied. After observing my tried-and-true method of packing, Jodi thought I needed a folding tutorial, a class I somehow missed in Dock Junction, Georgia. Without raising her voice, she showed me how to fold everything from underwear to shirts, but the most interesting part was her method for folding towels. It was life-changing. Jodi showed me that regardless of size, a rectangular towel could be folded longways twice. What's left got folded into three sections. Besides the visual appeal, towels folded this way stacked easily in the closet and were aesthetically pleasing. For a boy who didn't get out much, this was pure genius.

One bargain we made as a new couple was that each of us would leave the comfortable worlds we were accustomed to for one that did not yet exist, a risky choice on both sides. We agreed to forsake all others and how we learned to do things for the exciting opportunity to build a new life together with our own traditions and towel-folding methods. Since then, we've carefully woven the organization skills and sophisticated manners from the officer's quarters with the simple, relaxed customs of the sawmill.

To make our new life work, we divvied up household chores based on competence, not the limiting, gender-based binary descriptors that put men in charge of outside chores and women tending to those inside the home. There are some things I am good at doing and enjoy, but many more that I struggle with. It didn't take long for our new family to learn that banking, checkbooks, and numbers were not my strong suit. A few bounced checks (I never remembered to document the checks I wrote) were sufficient evidence that I needed to pass this responsibility to my wife, who's a lot more meticulous than I am.

As it turns out, banking is no more a man's job than cooking is woman's work. To my good fortune, Jodi is also a far superior cook, and I discovered I didn't have to surrender my Man Card if I washed dishes. In fact, according to a hand-printed sign I saw, it may prolong life. The sign read, "No man has ever been shot by a woman while washing dishes." Over the years, I've also picked up enough laundry secrets to keep relatively clean clothes in my closet, even if a few are discolored.

Jodi and I have discovered that together, we are much stronger and more capable than we are individually. Neither Mama nor the colonel would fully approve of how we've organized our lives, but it's worked for us. As Tevye taught us in *Fiddler on the Roof*, traditions are highly personal ways of organizing our lives together that make sense and help us keep balanced. Without them, Tevye says, "our lives would be as shaky as a fiddler on the roof!"

Section III

NOTES ON *CLEAVING*: MARRIED LOVE'S SECOND PRIMARY INGREDIENT

"This is now bone of my bones, and flesh of my flesh; she shall be called Woman . . ." Therefore shall a man leave his father and his mother and shall cleave unto his wife: and they shall be one flesh.
—Genesis 2:23, 24

Overview

The Genesis writer was clear on what it takes to build and maintain a healthy marriage and keep a big pot of love simmering. Plainly and up front, he unveiled the two mandates in fully loving another—leaving and cleaving—and Jesus echoed them in the New Testament (Matthew 19:5–6). These are the two primary ingredients in the love pot.

Generally, all the sound advice we so freely offer marriage candidates before the big day can be categorized in two ways: how to be a good *leaver* or a good *cleaver*. For many reasons, some of which I outlined in the previous section, the order is important. Cleaving follows the potentially painful first step of leaving the familiar people, places, and things for the promises inherent in becoming "bone of my bone, and flesh of my flesh."

The implication seems to be that to be a good cleaver, one must first be a good leaver. As your favorite uncle or aunt might put it, "You have to cut the apron strings before you can fully give yourself to the other."

As difficult as it is to turn your back on traditional ways of folding towels, making spaghetti, and celebrating holidays, the notion of welding two lives into one unit may be even scarier. It should be. After all, there are only two ways out of this high-stakes agreement—death or divorce—neither of which is pleasant to contemplate. A lifetime of loving and being loved unconditionally comes at a high cost. Sometimes conveniently, this second marriage ingredient of cleaving is often misunderstood or omitted as a modern requirement in marriage. After all, this dusty old admonition is at least 3,000 years old, and its promise of permanency seems to be out of step in this Snapchat age and planned obsolescence. However, Moses and I beg to differ. Cleaving is the bedrock of a solid marriage foundation and the stuff that keeps a fine-tuned relationship humming through the thick and thin.

In this section, I'll pick up the ancient word *cleaving*, brush it off, and hopefully help you rediscover its powerful implications in sticking people together at the marriage altar. A clear understanding of the strength of that bond is a key to building and maintaining a successful and happy marriage. However, for many who enjoy a good marriage, the essence of this old notion is familiar. As John put it, "I am not writing a new commandment to you … rather an old one you've had from the very beginning … that you love one another" (I John 2:7, NLT).

While a leaver is clearly one who leaves, a cleaver is not, at least in our language, generally associated with people sticking together for a lifetime. Part of the confusion is what my English teacher friends call cleaver's homonym. Unfortunately, *cleaver* conjures up images of someone wielding a large, heavy, rectangular, hatchet-type knife used to butcher animals. Primarily helpful with hacking through bone and muscle, a cleaver isn't typically associated with a candlelight dinner for two or long walks in the moonlight with your beloved.

Fortunately for lovers, there's a second definition of *cleaving* that will be explored later in this section. As will be evident, men and women must die in this tender version of *cleaving*, but it's not a horror story. Quite the opposite. Cleaving is sometimes painful but always powerfully transformative. In simple terms, it is the process of gluing one to the other. It is joining two imperfect people together at the deepest level, "bone of my bone, and flesh of my flesh," as Genesis put it. It is the ultimate human love story.

Cleaving was the old word for a lasting love that bends but doesn't break. However, in this fast-paced, screen-obsessed world designed around instant gratification and our tiny attention spans, it has lost its appeal. This section explores the industrial-strength glue that holds ragged men and women together through a lifetime of thick and thin, highs and lows, and sickness and health. This is expensive stuff that costs you everything you hold dear, including your life.

After leaving, cleaving is the second of love's two high-priced ingredients. A word of warning: This topic is not for immature readers and or folks who don't know sacrifice. However, it may help grownups more fully appreciate the personal costs that cleaving asks of lovers, empowering them to perhaps be better prepared for what Gibran called "the pain of too much tenderness." He further cautioned, "If you would seek only love's peace and love's pleasure . . . then it is better for you to pass out of love's threshing floor, into that seasonless world where you shall laugh, but not all of your laughter, and weep, but not all of your tears." Love is a serious obligation.

The problem, as I see it, is a shallow or naïve understanding of love, especially as it relates to marriage relationships. What it takes to fully love another cannot be purchased at a discount. This expensive four-letter word is a prerequisite in joining people together, but we're never quite sure how or what the implications, expectations, and real costs are. *Love* has been stretched to the point that its original meaning has been obscured or dismissed as old-fashioned and out of date in our everything-goes society. I think it's time to take another hard look at this powerful little word on which so much of our joy and contentment rest.

Most of us are keenly aware of the role of love in our lives, and some have a realistic appreciation for the weight of this little word. In the pages ahead, I'll share my own limited understanding of love and gladly invite you to share yours. The Scriptures are packed with similar love stories that sound like ours. What emerges from telling and retelling our love stories are valuable lessons on how this amazing gift is to be used. A deeper and fuller understanding of love, which connects us to each other and to our creator, is worthy of pursuit.

The metaphor I've used for love's mysterious powers is the ancient story of glue and its original formula (i.e., leaving and cleaving). However, over my educational career, I discovered that like my body and my old Volkswagen Beetle, metaphors break down when pushed too far. Most of the time my glue metaphor works, but occasionally love breaks free of the restraints imposed by language and soars to heights even the most apt metaphor cannot touch.

If you remember your fifth grade language arts class, you know *love* is a verb, something you do. Like any verb, it conveys action and can be conjugated and stretched to fit a variety of conditions and circumstances. In some uses, this serious four-letter word gets trivialized to the point of losing its meaning, escaping its restraints and posing as a noun—an almost wordless thing, feeling, or emotion. In these rare times, the noun rules are inadequate. *Love* was the only word that fit when I stood silently in my children's room and watched them sleep, when I found Jodi's note hidden in my suitcase, or when the two of us saw and heard Sandhill cranes flying over our cabin in a perfect V formation against a crisp blue autumn afternoon. The only combination of the twenty-six available letters that fit these and so many red-letter days in life was l-o-v-e. So, throughout this section, this little unruly word is sometimes a stark and demanding verb insisting something be done. At other times, it poses in its more elegant, softer form. In any of its incantations, love's power to change us remains mysterious.

At various times, love sneaks up on us, surprises us, and shocks us. Scripture is clear that when we follow the recipe closely, a satisfying, genuine product comes out of the oven. Though I don't know the chemistry and physics that break down the individual ingredients of bananas, oil, flower, sugar, and baking powder in the oven, I do know how alluring a warm slice of banana bread smells and tastes. However, all of that depends on putting the correct raw materials in the right proportions in the right conditions.

The chapters in this section examine cleaving's history, its high costs, and how—when mixed appropriately with leaving—it produces industrial-strength glue that sticks bone to bone and flesh to flesh. My hope is that a better understanding of this old tried and true recipe may help love-starved couples find a way forward. Maybe by putting handles on *love*, couples at the altar can learn to keep the fire burning for a lifetime. I believe that returning to love's fundamentals might also give serious lovers the ability to anticipate, identify, diagnose, and solve the inevitable issues that threaten lifelong, loving relationships.

Chapter 10

A BRIEF, STICKY HISTORY OF CLEAVING

Someday, after mastering the winds, the waves, the tides, and gravity,
we shall harness for God the energies of love, and then, for a second
time in the history of the world, man will have discovered fire.
—Pierre Teilhard de Chardin

THE BIBLE USES THE STRANGE old word *cleave* in the place of our modern word *love*. As I pointed out earlier, its homonym (think "meat cleaver") hasn't helped *cleave*'s PR campaign. Unless you're a fan of *Sweeney Todd*, it's no surprise that *cleave* is one of *love*'s least popular synonyms. "I cleave to you" is a much more sober and demanding way to say "I love you." There's little wonder why *cleave*, the original word that united Adam and Eve, is rarely used in polite society.

One red-letter event where you're likely to hear the old word *cleave* or its derivatives is a church wedding. In most other settings, *love* is the word of choice for describing and defining the fuzzy emotion between two people who really, really like each other. But what is love? Elizabeth Browning, Snoopy, and Elvis are just a few who made a good living off this very question. Ms. Browning suggests that the ways of love could be counted, whereas Snoopy claims, "Love is a warm puppy." The King of Rock and Roll, on the other hand, seems to understand the wonderful paradox of this simple little verb. He suggests that if he ever lost his love, he would be "looking back and longing for the freedom of my chains." Clearly there is some confusion as to how *love* and *cleaving* are connected. To better understand *love* it might help to trace its roots. A quick review of etymology—the study of word origins—might clear some of this up.

Cleave and *glue* have common origins, and both refer to the process of permanently attaching two objects—or in the case of this book, attaching two people formed from the dust of the earth (Genesis 2:7–9). Not surprisingly, at least for leavers and cleavers, our word *clay* is also tangled up in the origins of *cleaving* and *gluing*. As far back as the sixteenth century, the Latin *agglutinatus* ("to fasten with glue") was used to describe the relationship between two people. If those two people were particularly close, they were said to be "united as by glue."

Originally, *cleaving* grew out of the Old English word *clifian*, meaning "stick fast or adhere" (*Online Dictionary of Etymology*, 2017). In the thirteen century, the French added the word *gluier* to mean "to join or fasten together," particularly with a thick "viscous adhesive substance." Sticking things together was of particular interest to the artisans of the day who made utensils for everyday use. The raw material for these products was often the dirt under their feet, or what the Old Saxons called *klei*. They learned that when wet, the stiff, sticky, earth could be molded into pots and a host of other useful things. The potters of that day knew something (*slip* as we now know it) held pliable earth together during the molding process and through the fiery oven that made the pot useful. From there, words for *clay* and *stick together* were introduced.

At least 2,000 years before Christ, our ancestors were acquainted with methods for bonding wood and other materials together using boiled-down leftovers from butchered animals. These early artisans were not aware of the chemical and physical properties of this early form of glue, but they learned that when this concoction was spread over two properly fitted joints, the two bonded pieces became stronger and more flexible than either piece was before. This opened the possibilities of creating beds, shelves, and pots that became indispensable building blocks of communal living.

As these insights were passed to new generations, some smart chap named this magical substance. The Old English word *glew* describes the thick, sticky stuff produced from boiling large animal parts, such as hooves, hide, and bones. As it turns out, most of us would recognize the by-product of this grizzly butchering process as an early form of Elmer's Glue. Thanks to Elmer, even kindergartners know what this sticky stuff can do. However, I'm not sure adults at the marriage altar understand the powerful imagery and implications undergirding marriage.

Chapter 11

LOVE: A ONE-WAY TRIP TO THE GLUE FACTORY

"[W]hosoever will lose his life for my sake, shall find it . . ."
—Matthew 16:25

EVER SINCE ARITHMETIC TAUGHT US the advantages of partnership (two is better than one when raising children, gathering food, and building a sustainable life), poets, songwriters, and moviemakers have tried to describe the bond that ties us to each other and to the Almighty. After exhausting some old phrases, we have settled on the short word *love*. We mostly agree that loving relationships offer more than simple practical advantages. They give existence meaning and purpose and help organize our lives. Jesus underscored this point, declaring that the sum of our responsibilities on earth fit into one of two major categories—loving others and loving God. That sounds simple enough, but we often overlook the price of this love that binds us to each other and our creator.

Over time, different cultures have tried several other terms, other than our catchall *love*. If you ever earned a star for Sunday School attendance, you probably know the Greeks have at least six words for it, each highlighting a different type of love. Roman Krznaric (2023) lists them as the following:

- *Eros* or passion
- *Phila* or friendship
- *Ludus* or playful
- *Agape* or what C.S. Lewis called "Christian love for everyone"
- *Pragma* or a longstanding love
- *Philautia* or love of self.

The Old English word *lufu* and its Sanskrit derivative, *lubhyati,* are loosely translated "desires." *Libet* is Latin for "it is pleasing." Each of these notions contributes to our understanding of love; however, if we peel away these layers of meaning, there are fundamental ingredients that unify our understanding of this mysterious four-letter word that knits humans together and, by extension, to the Creator.

With overuse, the word *love* has become worn and diluted by our thoroughly modern sensibilities and impatience. It has been pulled and stretched to excuse poor decisions and explain inappropriate choices. It's also loosely thrown around to describe everything from paint colors to the "Stairway to Heaven" guitar riff. There is no hint of permanency in these frivolous uses of the seminal concept joining men and women to God and their spouse. Old pictures from back in the day are entertaining examples of how seasons of life change us and our tastes in fashion, hairstyles, and interior design. That spiffy lava lamp with the dark blue wall paint from college and the head-banging music I couldn't live without have thankfully had their day. Love as a temporary obsession is not the stuff of marriage vows intended to weather the inevitable changes that come with life. Neither is it an accurate description of the unbreakable bond with the Creator.

At least 3,000 years before Christ, folks knew something about sticking things together. Although the properties of the mysterious substance that stuck paper and sticks together were not fully understood, the ancients knew how to make it.

It's easy to see how and why the synthetic, transient notion of love is an attractive alternative for the love necessary for a firm marriage foundation. As poets and songwriters have shown us, *love* rolls off the tongue easily and has excellent rhyming potential. When paired with a catchy melody, it's fun to sing along with in the car. But the kind of love that sticks men and women together for a lifetime is a little more serious bubble-gum music. It is powerful and resilient, invaluable and rare. As Chaucer pointed out, that brand of love is a real, bone-deep feeling. It's neither frivolous nor temporary and certainly not cheap. Ultimately, it will cost all you have in this world.

The High Costs of Love

Each wedding participant and witness is a product of the earth, a piece of clay wonderfully shaped and molded. Like me and every member of my family, you are a bag of dirt into which God poured special stuff, but all of our bags leak and contain impurities. None of us is perfect, and according to Scripture, that condition will persist in life and marriage, "so long as you both shall live." So how can two flawed hunks of clay be permanently glued together in such a way that empowers you to endure the inevitable storms and stresses of stupid choices? Love. It is the industrial strength glue required for such a job, and it's hinted at in the very first mention of such a union in Genesis 2:23: "Bone of my bone and flesh of my flesh."

The power of such a union cemented with love can be demonstrated by gluing two boards together. Need directions? I found the step-by-step procedures outlined on the back of an old Elmer's Glue bottle in my garage. Elmer suggests that the two pieces must be clean, and the parts must fit together snuggly. Assuming the pieces are clean and fit together well, I must apply glue evenly over the two surfaces and then clamp the pieces together overnight. Following the gluing ceremony, the two boards are permanently mated. Excessive force may pull the two boards apart, but never neatly. Fragments of one board will forever be embedded in the other.

To produce glue that holds a couple together through thick and thin, the husband and wife must each lay themselves on the sacrificial altar. This high demand of marriage is a way of practicing the first requirement of love, the willingness to lay down your life for your best friend in the world (John 15:13). It is the ultimate sacrifice, and this is a large part of the covenanting performed at the marriage altar. God then collects the stuff that sticks bones to bone and flesh to flesh and applies it liberally. After being clamped together overnight, the two rise as one, united in holy matrimony. Jesus himself blessed this sacred union and warned, "What therefore God has joined together, let not man put asunder" (Mark 10:9).

Chapter 12

LOVE IS IN TENSE

If no love is, Oh God what fele I so?
—Francesco Petrarch, *Sonnet 102*

MOST OF THE TIME, *LOVE* is a verb that suggests we do something. However, it sometimes moonlights as a noun, especially on a warm spring night when walking with your sweetie as the stars dance so close you can almost touch them. In those tender moments, *love* is that achingly indescribable feeling when your darling reaches for your hand or straightens your collar. It is also the word for what your sweetie does that initiates the feeling. *Love* is the word we reach for when no other combination of letters is appropriate. In its noun form, love names the longing to be close to the beloved, and in its verb form, it answers to the question, "What can I do about it?" Love is what Renaissance poet Petrarch felt, driving him to his haunting question.

In all its forms, *love* has been softened by overuse and casual use. It's shoehorned into conversations about what we do for a living, Friday night football, and the sounds of waves crashing on the shore. That same little word also describes how we feel about family and God. It is easy to forget that this short, multipurpose word is rooted in the strict and often-severe verbs *leave* and *cleave*.

Maybe our ancestors were more precise in their use of language or better prepared to face the awesome responsibilities of caring deeply for another. Leaving and cleaving was the price they willingly paid, and their payment paid off. Their relationships, like a '56 Chevy pickup, were built to last. They were acquainted with our "better or worse" conditions, and their relationships could take a hit and keep on trucking. They seemed to know in their bones that the vows of love were not idle, but solemn promises made "in the presence of God and these witnesses." From their perspective, saying "I love you" indicated a willingness to leave all and cleave to one alone. Admittedly, that's not the most romantic view of love ever proposed, and I'm pretty sure that line will probably not be on your next anniversary card. However, it is the foundation of the glue that binds the hearts of men and women. For serious lovers, leaving and cleaving hold the secrets of how and why love lasts and—most importantly—how to make it.

Based on many stories—including my own—the early days of a relationship are marked by strange, palpable emotions based on attraction, mutual interest, or nameless feelings registering more in the heart than the head. For a variety of reasons (including a sprinkling of sound ones), some enamored folks are eventually convinced that their two hearts must be one and they say so in public. At the subsequent ceremony, the tenor of love that brought them together changes drastically.

The soft, squishy *love*—the warm emotions and gooey feelings—is rarely brought up in the ceremony. Instead, the officiant zeroes in on the decidedly unromantic verb tense of *love*. The minister reminds the marriage candidates of leaving and cleaving, a decidedly unsexy marriage foundation. Before declaring them husband and wife, the person in charge asks a few hard questions of the candidates and their will to love the other. If both promise to do the things love asks of them—to commit, communicate, understand, and submit—they are proclaimed as husband and wife.

Chapter 13

A LASTING LOVE

All that we love deeply becomes a part of us.

—Helen Keller

"Do you love this woman?"
I was surprised the preacher at my wedding didn't ask that obvious rhetorical question. Guess the answer was way too obvious. At our 1971 ceremony in the woods, Jodi walked down a winding path toward the altar as she wore a magnificent flowing white dress. A wreath of baby's breath flowers rested in her long blond hair, and she was the picture of drop-dead gorgeous. Of course I loved her. So, the minister opted for a more difficult set of questions in line with the solemnity of the occasion. "Gary," he said, "will you love this woman?" Before I could answer, he listed a few circumstances that have tested my decision over the last fifty-plus years. "Will you love her when she's young and when she's old," he said, "when she's sick and when she's well, when she's poor and when she's rich?" Cold sober and eager to ace the exam, I said "Yes!" Grace of grace, Jodi agreed to take me under the same conditions.

What united us were those very conscious promises to maintain when that abstract feeling that drew us together dimmed. Such a covenant bond is excessively strong compared to any bond based on fickle emotions and frivolous feelings. At times, white-hot emotions fire up between us, but not all the time. As all married folks know, emotions and feelings wax and wane. How we feel about anything is a personal construct built on a unique and singular view of the world. That feeling, created from information and evidence that is distorted by personal bias, is easily bruised by ill-chosen words or innocent facial expressions. The long and short of it, Jodi likes me better some days than others. However, no bad days negate the vow we made to love each other no matter what—a promise that includes my gum smacking and fingernail biting that, to this day, are just two sins that, like the Hebrews writer said, "doth so easily beset us" (Hebrews 12:1). The thing that joined Jodi and me is the verb form of *love*, a sincere promise to do something about those squishy feelings that attracted us to each other, even when we don't feel like it.

Making love is a loaded phrase relegated to the bedroom and is not something we generally talk about in polite company. When we can find words to fit this narrowly defined private experience, they usually include modifiers like *beautiful* or *embarrassing*. Rarely do we describe lovemaking as mundane acts of the will we do routinely and sometimes sacrificially. The common misunderstanding is that we have little control over love. We too easily dismiss our role in loving another. We prefer to think of love as something we fall into in the back seat of a Chevy or some emotion that sneaks up on us in a dimly lit theater. Loving another, however, is no accident. Everyday activities done freely and without prompts, like taking out the trash, hanging up a shirt, complimenting our spouse, and washing dishes preheat the oven to cook up something special later. Love's various verb tenses are not always easy, soft, or tender, but neither is the process of making a love that sticks ragged, imperfect people together over time.

Love provides both the glue and grease of human relationships. Grownups know or suspect that a lasting love isn't built on emotions and feelings that depend on circumstances, time of day, or surrounding events. Such flimsy unions can be undone by bad breath, a lousy day at work, a faulty memory, or an endless list of thinly veiled excuses. Unlike emotions and feelings, the solemn vows at the marriage altar cannot be taken back or negated by circumstance. It is that agreement, that "I will take you and you will take me warts and all" that provides the rock-solid foundation of marriage and is the source of the ooey-gooey feeling that couples enjoy most of the time.

We, especially us men, like to boast that we would gladly take a bullet for our beloved. That's a safe claim to make, because the likelihood of that happening is almost zero. However, there are lots of opportunities every day to lay your life down, to sacrifice your desires, to hit the pause button on your priorities and do something special for or with your beloved, just because. These random acts of kindness are natural lovemaking sessions in which you whip up a fresh batch of the adhesive that sticks bone to bone and flesh to flesh. They require no pills, no money, and very basic skills. You can also leave your hat and your clothes and shoes on, and you won't have to hide to do it. There are no age limits or expiration dates on kindness. Although it should not be the motivation, I can testify that the reward for these selfless acts is that you will get back more than you ever gave. The residual benefits last forever and ever, amen.

Section IV

NOTES ON THE SECONDARY INGREDIENTS THAT MAKE LOVE WORK

What a strange machine man is! You fill him with bread, wine, fish, and radishes, and out of him comes sighs, laughter, and dreams.
—*Zorba the Greek* by Nikos Kazantzakis

Overview

By now, you are aware that leaving and cleaving are the two primary ingredients in homemade married love. However, as I learned in my banana-bread fiasco, there's more to this story. If you're interested in making a fresh batch of love, there are a few other ingredients that are less important but essential nonetheless. These secondary ingredients act as blending, lubricating, and binding agents, breaking down the natural sugars in the two primary ingredients. The result is a batch of homemade married love with enhanced flavor and texture.

The two chapters in this section suggest a behavioral model of how this process might look on paper and a handy guide that details how the role players work their magic. My hope is that you gain insights into the scriptural obligation to make love or as Paul put it, "render due benevolence" (I Corinthians 7:3). Additionally, I hope you will see that "fulfilling the marital duty" (as the NIV translated I Corinthians 7:3) is not relegated to the bedroom. I have learned that most of the lovemaking process takes place in the daylight when fully clothed. Raking leaves, paying bills, washing dishes, arranging a date night, and countless other everyday actions can be expressions of commitment, communication, understanding, and submission that make the obligations to leave and cleave so much sweeter.

Chapter 14

HOW LOVE MIGHT LOOK ON PAPER: A MODEL

He who has a why to live can bear almost any how.
—Friedrich Nietzsche

THOUGH MY BAKING CAREER WAS short, I learned from it. If you want to make banana bread, you need the right ingredients. The two essentials are right there in the title: lots of bananas and flour (even I know this is the main ingredient in bread). But the fine print in the recipe I used listed a supporting cast of players (see the list below), players I thought weren't as important as the two stars, bananas and flour. My thinking went something like this: Get the two stars right and everything else will fall into place. As it turns out, little things matter.

A Banana Bread Recipe
   4 ripe bananas, mashed
   2 cups all-purpose flour
   1 teaspoon baking powder
   ½ teaspoon salt
   2 large eggs
   ⅔ cup white sugar

As I admitted previously, I got a lot of little things right, but I couldn't tell the difference between baking powder and powdered sugar. The recipe only called for a teaspoon, so I figured it wasn't too important. It was. As I recently learned from my smart computer,

> Baking powder is made up of sodium bicarbonate (baking soda), an acidic component (usually cream of tartar), and a filler like cornstarch to prevent premature reaction. When mixed with liquid, the acid and base react, releasing carbon dioxide gas, which gets trapped in the batter, creating bubbles that expand during baking. Most commercially available baking powders are "double-acting," meaning they release a first burst of gas when mixed with liquid and a second burst when exposed to heat in the oven. (AI Overview)

Yes, that tiny teaspoon makes a huge difference. That complex white stuff, baking powder, acts like a chemical catalyst to break down the two big stars of the recipe and makes the final product desirable.

Likewise, leaving and cleaving need a little help, an agent that gets them together and makes the pair better than either can be alone. Neither leaving without cleaving nor cleaving without leaving establishes a good foundation for married love. It takes both and a few other ingredients, perhaps a pinch of baking powder (not powdered sugar), to create a love that sticks two hearts together.

When a spouse says, "My partner doesn't love me," knowing how that might be fixed is no easy task. A guide for diagnosing and resolving relational problems would be helpful, especially if we focused on what a lover does that generates feelings of love or abandonment.

Later in this chapter, I offer a behavioral model that I think plays the role of baking powder and other secondary ingredients in a homemade love recipe. This model may explain some of the things that make leaving and cleaving work and how to make a better batch of love when it's obvious that something in the recipe has been omitted. However, first we need a refresher on our collective history and use of models.

A Brief History of Model Making

Models are smaller, cheaper versions of the real thing. They describe or explain phenomena that may not be directly observable or accessible. By manipulating elements in the model, we can better understand why things work or don't work. Because models are objects and not real people, they don't get their feelings hurt and they don't pout. The more accurate the model, the better it is in making predictions, diagnosing problems, and planning treatment options. It can also suggest ways to prevent problems that would hinder the smooth operation of whatever real thing the model represents. Models undergird our understanding of everything from the vastness of the universe to why we are both like everyone else and wholly unique. The DNA model is a good example.

On a cold and blustery Saturday afternoon in February 1958, American biologist James Watson stood in The Eagle Pub in Cambridge, England, and announced to the late lunch crowd that he and his British partner, Francis Crick, had "discovered the secret of life." Indeed, these two brash, young scientists had something to be excited about. They found the keys that unlocked the secret of our common genetic code, one of the twentieth century's most important discoveries—how the chain of repeating units of deoxyribonucleic acid (DNA) creates each human's genetic fingerprint.

This complicated genetic code contains clear instructions for the process that unfolds throughout an individual person's life. Exact specifications for succeeding generations are passed on as part of a family's inheritance, from Mom's curly hair or Dad's blue eyes to the cleft in Grandpa's chin or Grandma's ear for music. Each of us has trillions of these microscopic instructional manuals that explain who we are at the exclusion of everyone else, how we are like some who share our genes, and how we have things in common with everyone in our branch on the family tree. Fans of CSI (pick a city) know we leave traces of this evidence everywhere we go, through our touch, our blood, our hair, and more. High schoolers learn that these tiny copies of instructions can be read and, under the right conditions, rats, sheep, roses, and fruit flies can be cloned from corresponding DNA in the lab.

Watson and Crick clearly stumbled on something big, but it was not DNA. At least a decade earlier, Linus Pauling, Oswald Avery, Rosalind Franklin, and Maurice Wilkins worked on the idea of DNA molecules, but no one knew how they functioned. All they knew was that inside the nucleus of countless cells in the human body resided twenty-three pairs of chromosomes in some combination of X and Y that identified gender and much, much more. On each chromosome they noticed evidence of DNA molecules that seemed important, but its purpose remained fuzzy.

It was an idea without a picture, no universally accepted image to explain how DNA's complex structure worked. So, Watson and Crick took their colleagues' ideas and proposed a model that illustrated how these tiny structures were put together and how these microscopic building blocks of life might look. They envisioned two strands of nucleotides as two sides of a twisted or spiral staircase, with steps of genetic code written in some combination of Adenine (A), Thymine (T), Guanine (G), and Cystosine (C). It was a moment of great clarity.

This picture or model opened the curtain on some of life's greatest mysteries and spurred even more important discoveries. From there, Francis Collins, a devout Christian, led the team that mapped the human genome. His team's work has since saved lives by improving diagnosis of disease, detection of genetic predispositions to disease, and targeting therapy for specific individuals. It has also been the reason many of us know more about where we came from and how we're connected by spitting into a tube. Indeed, what a strange machine man is.

The more Collins discovered about what he called "the language of God," the stronger this decorated scientist's faith became. As impressive as science's ability to better understand how life works, Collins (2007) insists it

> does not tell us what it means to be human. In my view, DNA sequence alone, even if accompanied by a vast trove of data on biological function, will never explain certain special human attributes, such as the knowledge of the Moral Law and the universal search for God. Freeing God from the burden of special

acts of creation does not remove him as the source of the things that make humanity special, and of the universe itself. It merely shows us something of how he operates.

Collins's inspirational insights into how God operates were made possible by men and women before him who tried and mostly failed to understand DNA's critical role in the design of life. Particularly important was the double helix model Watson and Crick proposed for the structure of DNA. This physical representation of DNA quickened further discovery, proof that the common strategy of model building is immediately useful, especially in science.

Models are equally popular in everyday life. Toys like plastic lawn mowers, Easy-Bake Ovens, Betsy Wetsy dolls, and Tonka trucks are all models—smaller, cheaper versions of the real thing. Their scaled down, simplified design teaches serious lessons about how the real world works, while softening the consequences of mistakes. A wreck with a Mack truck and VW on I-75 is a lot different than the collision of a Tonka truck and Hot Wheels Corvette on the living room floor.

In the adult world, serious grown men and women play with models to learn how building materials might fare in an earthquake or how to save a life with CPR. Copernicus used models to explain his radical idea that the sun was at the center of our solar system. By manipulating objects representing the "heavenly bodies" (e.g., earth, moon, and sun), he could demystify seasonal changes, eclipses, and time differences with rational explanations. He could even make predictions regarding each. When Apollo 13 pilot Jim Lovell declared, "Houston, we have a problem," the issue was diagnosed and a temporary fix arranged in the capsule model here on earth using a one-to-one model of the Lovell's spacecraft.

In fashion, figuring out what's trending can make or break a designer. Upcoming and established designers test hunches by draping their goods on models slightly larger than a coat hanger and having them parade down a runway. The model's exaggerated walk demonstrates how the fabric moves and hangs, and that 1,000-yard stare hints at just how serious the fashion business should be taken.

When Watson and Crick interrupted the lunch crowd at the Eagle Pub, they were introducing their new model of a DNA molecule that helped others see how tightly wound microscopic strands of life fit together. The double helix model explained how so many tiny bits of life (forty-six pairs of DNA—twenty-three original chromosomes and a copy, each about six nanometers or six billionths of a meter in size) could be squished into the nucleus of a cell. Watson and Crick's model was shared widely and made many other advancements possible, including Collins's team mapping the human genome.

A Model of Love's Ingredients

I am not saying the Behavioral Model of Leaving and Cleaving (Figure 1) is on par with Watson and Crick's announcement, far from it. Watson and Crick are real scientists, while I'm just a curious old teacher. Unlike their model of DNA, the picture on the next page isn't a replica of love, but a preliminary sketch of how love's primary and secondary ingredients are related. With all due respect, the mysterious stuff that glues one human being to another is more difficult to isolate, study, and write about than DNA. Most of what we know about love is based on what we see, feel, and experience, and those perceptions differ between us.

Like Watson and Crick, I didn't invent or discover the substance at the heart of the model in question. It's been there all along. Like Watson and Crick, I simply have a curiosity about the powerful force that shapes every facet of life. And as Watson and Crick were not the first to detect or isolate DNA, I know that neither I nor Huey Lewis and the News invented or discovered the power of love.

After listening to countless love songs, reading loads of love poems, and sitting through more than my share of sappy Hallmark movies, I was still a little fuzzy on the concept of love. The slippery thing just won't fit in a simple combination of nouns and verbs. So, I turned to old wives' tales, hoping for a clear picture. After all, a picture could save you and me at least 1,000 words. If the old wives were right, the picture below should simplify love, eliminating a few thousand words and making life easier for slow readers like me. Do note, if you're planning on cooking up a batch right away, it's a good idea to preheat the oven, but you probably don't need me to tell you how. Also, I labeled the ingredients to make sure your batch turns out better than my banana bread.

The picture below (Figure 1) identifies the primary and secondary ingredients in a homemade pot of love. When these ingredients are properly blended and the result evenly applied, it forms a lasting bond between two imperfect human beings. As we both know, imperfect people do imperfect things, creating problems that threaten even the healthiest bonds of love. When love loses its grip, the model offers guidance in making a fresh supply at home. For those willing to pay, the model provides a shopping list and implicit instructions for brewing a fresh pot of homemade love. I offer the model with the hope that it helps demystify the mysterious stuff that explains why we stick together through thick and thin.

It seems that marital love is a function of leaving and cleaving, the two primary ingredients in love's recipe. The better a couple is at these two fundamentals, the richer and deeper the glue that unites them. Those who backslide on their vows "to leave all others" and "to cleave only to

Figure 1: A Behavioral Model of Leaving & Cleaving

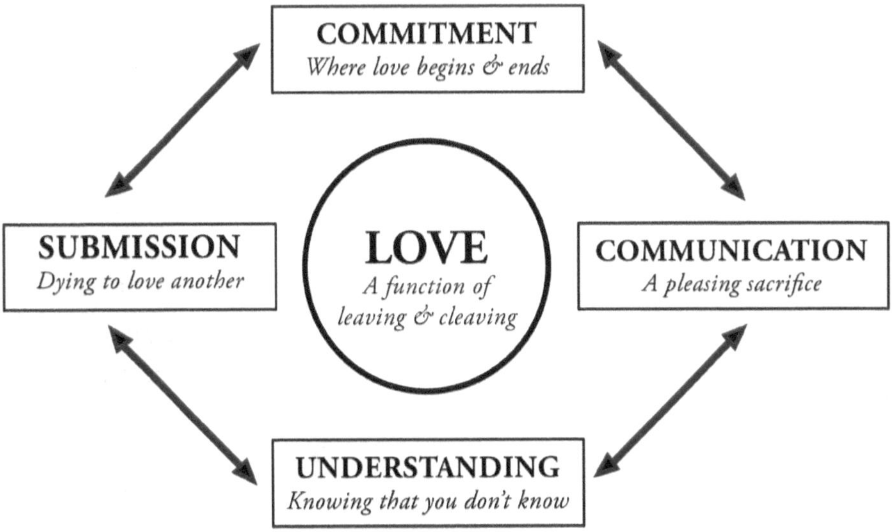

COMMITMENT
Where love begins & ends

SUBMISSION
Dying to love another

LOVE
A function of leaving & cleaving

COMMUNICATION
A pleasing sacrifice

UNDERSTANDING
Knowing that you don't know

this one" may find their relationship falling apart. In Sections II and III, we discussed these basics in depth and how they are related. However, leaving and cleaving need other, smaller ingredients in the mixing bowl to make the two stars of the recipe shine. These secondary ingredients—commitment, communication, understanding, and submission—act like baking powder, butter, eggs, salt, and sugar in the banana bread recipe.

The model is based on four assumptions.

1. Couples who are fully committed to each other will communicate.

2. Couples who communicate regularly will better understand one another.

3. Couples who more completely understand one another are more willing to submit or "prefer the other."

4. Couples who are willing to submit or deny themselves out of deference for the other find it easier to commit to one another.

When mixed with a willingness to leave and cleave, commitment, communication, understanding, and submission act like the secondary ingredients in a recipe. They set the conditions that allow the two primary ingredients—leaving and cleaving—to do their work. As a result, the mixture rises, flavors blend, individual particles bind together, and the whole thing sweetens. Though these secondary ingredients seem small and insignificant compared to the Big Two, as my banana bread experience proves, a relationship without one or more of these four supporting ingredients will fall flat.

Uses for a Model of Love

The secondary ingredients in love's recipe—commitment, communication, understanding, and submission—are connected in a specific and sequential pattern, with one leading to the next. Problems in one are related to unsatisfactory performance in the previous, so that issues with commitment lead to an unwillingness to submit, and a lack of understanding may find its root in poor communication. These secondary ingredients support the two primary demands of loving—leaving and cleaving, softening their hard edges and creating an environment in which participants willingly choose to leave and cleave.

There are at least four uses of such a model. First, the model is built on a behavioral description of love's lesser, but essential ingredients. Identifying these components offers marriage candidates and therapists a way to talk about the abstract connective tissue that binds married couples. Second, the model can help sharpen the focus on specific problems that are likely related to perceived or real manifestations of deficits in commitment, communication, understanding, or submission. Third, reducing issues to a clearly defined root cause improves behavioral problem-solving outcomes. Last, the Behavior Model of Leaving and Cleaving can help marriage candidates prepare for the deadly serious proposition of marriage. This kind of preventative maintenance gives couples the confidence, as the song says "to face unafraid the plans that we made."

Beyond Tonka trucks' entertainment value and fashion models' cute factor, there are many other ways paper and pencil models serve us. With minimal risk and expense, they put names on objects in whatever phenomena we aim to understand and can indicate how objects in the model relate. As we better understand the objects within a model, we learn about their beginning and ending points and why and how the phenomena works. Additionally, a good model illustrates ways we can proactively prevent bad things from happening. Let me explain.

Love Handles

It's almost impossible to talk about something without a name. One of Sigmund Freud's major contributions was naming and defining what he saw as three principle parts of the psyche: the id, ego, and superego. Once these concepts had a name, Freud could talk about them with others and offer plausible explanations for silly and sometimes self-destructive behaviors. For instance, he explained the tendency to continually find a particular fault in others as an unconscious defense mechanism he called *projection*, an attempt to bolster the ego (our view of self). He argued that because we're generally unwilling to admit our faults, we tend to point out that very fault in others. If you have a problem with greed, you tend to find others greedy. Before Freud, we simply said, "The devil made me do it" or "I couldn't help myself." Neither is true, and neither suggests a fix.

By putting handles on the slippery concept of love in its many forms, it's easier to discuss love and understand how it might be shored up. By defining *love* as "leaving and cleaving," lovers are empowered to commit, communicate, understand, and submit. Commitment is a first step to accepting the seriousness of the marriage contract. If you don't fully appreciate what you're vowing to do, you're unlikely to recognize threats to the relationship or how to overcome these threats. Giving threats a name can make them easier to manage.

Marriage should not be built on a flawed understanding of love pieced together from a catchy song, rom-com, or a magazine's ten-question quiz on compatibility. As you learned in Sunday School, marriages constructed on these shifting sands are likely to have a sad ending when the rain comes. Real love is rock solid, resilient, and sometimes inconvenient. Giving name to love's components makes it possible to diagnosis what makes the relationship work or fail. For married folks, that provides abiding comfort and joy.

Problem-Solving

One of my favorite preachers, Dorlan Queener, said we tend to treat first and diagnose second, a version of the "Ready, fire, aim!" leadership philosophy. Our model offers a handy way to fix that kind of thinking, so we solve problems that need solving. If the marriage relationship shows signs of distress, the first place to look is in the two main ingredients, leaving and cleaving. Leaving issues are not cleaving issues and vice versa. However, leaving precedes cleaving in the recipe—don't forget! And be assured, bad leavers are rarely good cleavers.

Narrowing the problem down to these primary ingredients is a good start, but you're still a long way from home. There are thousands of hints that indicate leaving is the issue. Having to touch base with parents on minor decisions, an unwillingness to fold towels a new way, and failing to make your bed because you didn't have to at home are just a few warning signs. Indications that cleaving is the source of the problem are just as numerous. The difference is that these symptoms point to problems in the supply of the glue that holds the family together. A lack of romance, frequent excuses to be away, and showing little interest in the spouse's day-to-day routine are a few signs that the husband or wife or both need to get back in the kitchen and whip up a fresh batch of love.

As with leave and cleave, the secondary ingredients of commitment, communication, understanding, and submission implicitly suggest solutions to common problems in one or more of the catalysts of love. While it's impossible to resolve the countless ways couples can unravel, a study of the four secondary ingredients is a good place to start.

Problems, including the Big Three (sex, money, and in-laws) are symptoms and expressions of deeper issues rooted in love's ingredients. Issues regarding frequency of sex, spending habits, and choosing where to spend holidays could be rooted in commitment, communication, understanding, or submission or incomplete leaving or ineffective cleaving. If one spouse's spending habits are rooted in a lack of commitment, putting him or her on a budget won't fix things. Budgets may save you money, but they won't correct a lack of commitment. Resolving a marriage problem requires a close examination of the root cause, not the symptom. On the plus side, I don't know of any marital problem that can't be solved (or at least better managed) with significant increases in commitment, communication, understanding, and submission or a renewed vow to be a better leaver and cleaver.

Understanding the Basics

Any issue strong enough to threaten a relationship affects both parties. A lasting repair of that breach will require both to participate in the resolution, a hard bargain to strike when emotions are high and wounds are deep. In my experience helping couples navigate perilous times, I've learned that one-sided fixes don't last. However brief the fix, the pain endures. Some of you on the other side of my word processor are personally acquainted with the almost unbearable heartache of being ripped apart from another. You already know that healing and restoration may take a lot of time and endless baby steps. For those who've known what Gibran called "the pain of too much tenderness," my message is to keep the faith. I have it on good authority and written in red ink by one who should know that faith the size of a mustard seed can move mountains (Matthew 17:20). Frederick Buechner's definition of faith provides yet another handhold for brokenhearted believers. He taught that faith is knowing, way down at the bottom of your troubled, beating heart, that the worst thing that can happen is never the last thing (Buechner, 1993).

Preventive Maintenance

Grandma was right when she said, "Honey, a stitch in time saves nine," because prevention truly is the best policy. Surprisingly, Grandma wasn't the first to say so. Her advice echoes that of sixteenth-century diplomat Niccolo Machiavelli. Machiavelli was charged with preparing a prince to be king and in one session stated that the prince must pay close attention to his people. He advised that a revolution is hard to detect in its earliest days, but easiest to cure. Ignore the warning signs and any fool can detect the full-blown revolution, which becomes increasingly difficult to fix. Married people know the truth of his advice. Ignore little things at your peril. Very quickly, inconsequential disagreements over restaurant choices can escalate into full-blown skirmishes that can inflict mortal wounds on the relationship.

It's not uncommon to hear friends talk about "working on their marriage." The problem with "work plans" is that they are often, like the ill-defined love that joined them, too abstract. Nitpicky solutions fix symptoms but don't address root causes. It's like shoving an old scarf in a kid's mouth to cure a hacking cough. At first, the disturbing noise is muffled to a manageable level, and the solution seems to be working. But soon, the kid's simmering anger boils over. He yanks the scarf out and starts screaming. Treating symptoms without examining the root doesn't actually fix much. Hasty solutions can also introduce unintended consequences that can be more troublesome than the original issue. Resolving to only smoke outside, make the bed every morning, or keep the car running needs a strong purpose for the behavior to stick. The old recipe for love offers a way to diagnose relationship problems and suggests solutions.

I've used this model of making love to guide struggling couples toward solutions to problems that threatened to rip them apart. In some cases I was successful, but in others, the deep wounds inflicted by deficits in commitment, communication, understanding, and submission were fatal. I also found the model useful in premarital counseling. In that setting, couples explore tools pulled from the four secondary ingredients that have, anecdotally at least, helped spouses negotiate rough patches in their marriages. In my experience, successful couples are those who repeatedly test the hypothesis that "an ounce of prevention is worth a pound of cure" and come away with evidence to support that claim. Above all, the model is a reminder that the process of making the glue that sticks a couple together is neither cheap nor easy.

Chapter 15

A USER'S GUIDE

"When all else fails, read the directions."

—My Wife, Jodi

THE OVERSIMPLIFIED MODEL OF LOVE in the previous chapter is based on an old recipe for "bone of my bone, and flesh of my flesh." The model suggests that, with the right ingredients on hand, true love can be homemade. If the model is accurate, couples beginning a relationship can stock up on ingredients to sustain marriage over the long haul, couples running low on their supply of love can restock, and established partners can put away stores of love's ingredients as a hedge against times of want.

That sounds simple enough, but for novices like me, it's not. Those of us who aren't mechanically minded and are bad cooks need step-by-step instructions, a user's guide to the model. The picture of Betty Crocker holding a tasty-looking cake on the cake mix box isn't enough. Although I don't like it, I have to follow the steps on the box explicitly if I expect the finished product to look anything like the blue-ribbon-winning cake on the package. It's so aggravating that my mama never had to read instructions, despite making cakes all her adult life.

As I've said repeatedly, this idea has been around for centuries. People have loved and been loved for as long as our species has walked the planet. We have also seen others willfully and blatantly destroy some of God's favorite children. Over time, these lovers and haters have been our teachers, and we have learned their lessons, mostly secondhand. For the last 2,000 years, an old book on relationships and the glue that binds one to another has been widely available. The big story from Genesis to Revelations is that God loves us and we should in turn love each other. To do that, some of us need more instructions.

The model of love (Figure 1) is grounded in the instructions I dug out of that old book. The two primary ingredients, leaving and cleaving, are from the Genesis account regarding the original design of marriage, and the secondary ingredients—commitment, communication, understanding, and submission—come from other passages in the same book. My model simply puts these puzzle pieces together in a way that describes what lovers do.

What Lovers Do

Assuming the conditions *of leaving and cleaving* have been met, there are four additional supporting ingredients that make these two giant issues in love work. These four—*commitment, communication, understanding,* and *submission*—help create the conditions to brew up a hearty brand of love that will literally stick to your ribs. I've discovered that when blended in the right order and proper heat is applied, the resulting concoction will knock your socks off and give you the strength to hold on when the heavy winds and disappointments blow in and out of your relationship.

Lovers Commit

Love seems to begin with commitment, the conscious pledge of one's *troth*, the Middle English word for allegiance, fidelity, faithfulness, and loyalty. This covenant is the bedrock of connection between men and women and helps explain the die-hard link some have with organizations, causes, and movements. Some are fully committed to the Green Bay Packers, others to the country club, and some to punk rock. Along with this ride-or-die attachment comes an identity, complete with a uniform, code of behavior, and jargon understood by like-minded, sold-out companions. I've seen grown men and women wear cheese hats to a ball game. I watched people who seem to know instinctively which fork goes with the dessert. I've also been around some who wear safety pins in their eyebrow. Like their married brothers and sisters, these folks are fully committed. Whatever *it* is, their lives revolve around *it*, and *it* is a reliable guide in the individual's decision making. People who are committed are into *it* with all their heart.

Commitment is a ten-letter word that can serve as a summation of the old word *love*. Though the noun version of *commitment* is robust, the verb form—"to commit"—is even stronger. "I love you" is easy to say and almost expected at a housewarming or retirement party. However, "I am committed to you" has a more sober and lasting ring, reflecting the notion of cleaving to another, come what may. In a society built on transactional relationships, the softer, easier *love* is preferred by many. But joining two souls that "no man can put asunder" (Matthew 19:6) is a much more serious proposition demanding a much stronger word.

There is little mystery why *commitment* was replaced by the lighter, fluffier *love*. The implications of *commitment* are more serious than most are comfortable with, and—sin of sins—its derivatives are hard to rhyme in songs and poems. "I Commit to You Truly" and "How do I commit to thee? Let me count the ways" don't roll off the tongue with the ease of the daintier *love*-centric versions. Besides, the more somber tone and *commitment's* forever connotation could be offensive. And if you're selling records or anniversary cards, you don't want to offend or upset potential customers. They're always right, so they set the mark for what's acceptable.

However, the ceremony at the marriage altar is no frivolous affair. The two joined in holy matrimony must be willing to lay down their lives to create the adhesive that sticks them together. There is no better word to describe this selfless act than *commitment*, the first of four secondary ingredients in enduring love. Whether or not it rhymes or is offensive to our tender sensibilities should not be an issue. What matters is that the two marriage candidates know full well the costs of what Gibran called "love's peace and love's pleasure." Marriage demands those who would fully love another to commit everything to the union. Making that kind of love begins with the fullest measure of commitment, love's binding agent.

Lovers Communicate

The next ingredient that goes into the love pot is communication. The definition for the rawest verb form of *to communicate* is "to make common" human insights, feelings, dreams, and ideas. From a purely physical point of view, this is literally impossible and indispensable. It's no wonder communication is often reported as one of the biggest stumbling blocks couples face on the road to marital bliss and the cause of breakdowns in a wide variety of human relationships.

Committed people stay in constant contact with the object of their obsession. Because they keep up, real Packers fans are fully aware of the starting quarterback's health condition. If you want to know if the Dow is up today, I bet the guy with the tortoise-shell glasses at the country club is a better source than the girl in black with the safety-pin eye ornament. However, if you if you wanted to know where the tough Philadelphia punk rock band Sheer Mag is playing this weekend, check with the safety-pin princess. She'd know because she cares; and because she cares, she keeps up.

Communicating is about keeping up. For the obsessed, communication is a natural outgrowth of their commitment and leads directly to the third ingredient, understanding.

None of us gets it right all the time, but that doesn't bother true believers. Through trial and error and a willingness to learn about the other, these obsessed individuals develop a fuller understanding of the object of their affection. They gain intimate glimpses of the other that casual observers never see, building an understanding that reinforces the bond. Consequently, though communication is never perfect, it slowly builds layers of understanding that are resilient and resistant to outside forces that threaten the bonds of allegiance.

Important as it is, communication is literally impossible because we are unique individuals with an unrepeated set of experiences and preferences. If my pianist wife, Jodi, and I listen to a Chopin piano recording together, we take in the same notes but process them very differently. She hears things I don't. What I may find quite boring may leave her spellbound. We simply don't hear the same thing. She cringes when our church choir wanders off key, but that same sound pleases me. I don't hear what she hears. Across America, a similar scenario occurs every Sunday morning. We read the same Scriptures, but we can't agree on the meaning of specific passages. The sheer number of church brands that accommodate these differences is evidence of the lack of common ground. Other preferences in music, art, preaching, and sports teams make it clear that it's literally impossible "to make things common," but we can't stop trying.

Communication is a risky proposition with a high upside and very manageable downside. To be heard and acknowledged by another is a therapeutic ointment for our current epidemic of loneliness. It has the added distinction of making God smile. The writer of Hebrews speaks to all of us, especially married folk, when he wrote, "But do good and communicate, forget not for with such sacrifice God is well pleased" (13:16). Apparently, God is aware of how hard it is to communicate but also knows the blessing of communication for his struggling children, especially the married ones.

I have two homemade children I love dearly. If you want to do something nice for me, do something nice for my children. Spend some time with them, listen to their stories. Treat them as if they matter. Find out what they like to do, how they got interested in the jobs that pay their rent, their views on redemption—anything! As much as I love my babies, God loves his more. If you want to do God a big favor, pick out one of his favorite children (your spouse comes to mind) and spend some time finding out what that child of God is all about. Listen to that adult child's story and help lift some of the burden he or she carries. As you do, be warned that listening to another does not come naturally. The Hebrews writer was right—it's a sacrifice, a sacrifice that pleases God.

Good listening runs counter to how we're put together. We're hardwired to protect the loose collection of ideas of self we've stored over the years, and we'll defend that collection to the death and try desperately to make ourselves look good in the process. To focus for any length of time on another is unnatural and difficult. There are good reasons why therapists who listen to others for a living get paid more per hour than many Americans make in a day.

When we take a hack at communicating with another, it can quickly devolve into taking turns talking. It typically works like this. I ask you about your recent illness, and you launch into what happened. In the first few minutes of your story, I'm reminded of a similar time when I was sick. While I look intently at your face, I'm not listening. I'm rehearsing my own story in my head, getting the juicy details just right. Obviously, what happened to me is so much more important and entertaining than your lame account, so I can't wait till you finish. And you will be so impressed. At the first break in your story, I unleash my own enthralling tale, sure I have you hooked. But if you're like me, as I get my account, a little detail triggers a similar event in your life, and the roles reverse. Listening, however, is more than taking turns talking.

Truly listening is difficult, but not complicated. Listening requires two things most of us are incapable of doing:

1. Be there.
2. Shut up.

That sounds simple, but it's not. Being there means you are fully present, physically and mentally, and tuned into the speaker, focusing solely on him or her. Shutting up requires you to unplug the old video tapes in your head and concentrate on the speaker. We stop listening when we begin recounting our stories of similar events, and what could be a therapeutic experience becomes a conversation in which we take turns talking.

The sacrifice listening demands is often greater than we're willing to make. Good listeners are willing and courageous enough to deny themselves in deference to the other. Most of us have had someone—a therapist, friend, relative, pastor, or colleague—do exactly that for us in a time of deep need. When someone cares enough to stop, look, and listen to the garbled sentences rotting in our guts, the problems seem smaller, the issues more manageable, and the grief suddenly bearable.

Oodles of professional studies have examined characteristics of these listeners, and arguably the most prominent was Carl Rogers. In 1963, he reduced these individuals to three characteristics. He described good listeners, or *helpers* as he called them, as ordinary men and women who are:

1. **Empathetic/understanding.** They can put themselves in another's position and try to see the problem from the other's point of view.

2. **Genuine or real.** They are the same on the inside as they are on the outside, with nothing fake about them. Put simply, what you see is what you get.

3. **Respectful.** They don't dismiss, make fun of, or degrade the one to whom they listen.

Interestingly, what's not on Rogers's list are exclusion criteria for those who genuinely want to help. People of all ages and both genders from various educational, social, and financial backgrounds can excel or fail at listening. The big takeaway from Rogers's work, then, is that anyone can be a good listener. No office, beard, horned-rim glasses, couch, or framed degree hanging on the wall required.

My Uncle Carrol was such a helper. Though he had a long, fatal struggle with alcohol addiction and died a pauper, he was someone I went to when my world was caving in. He was understanding without being judgmental, a genuine human being who didn't try to be anybody else, and he respected me regardless of the venom I poured out. He was "an instrument of God's peace" in my life. Though he had plenty on his plate, Uncle Carrol gladly sacrificed what he was doing to listen to me.

We should not be shocked when communication doesn't work. There are so many ways it can and does breakdown. We may choose the wrong word, misread a facial expression, fail to accurately interpret what was said or done, or impose or project our feelings on the other. However, none of that should discourage us from fulfilling our obligation to try. Because sometimes, we get it right. To communicate requires the courage to bear the high costs of failure and a willingness to deny self in deference to the other. Though it may be impossible to fully understand the feelings and emotions of our closest neighbors (a.k.a. our spouses), it is imperative to continually work at it, a sacrifice that is well pleasing to God. Even our worst attempts at talking and listening nurture some level of understanding—one of the major reasons communication is an ingredient in the glue that holds fatally flawed humans together.

Lovers Understand

A better understanding of another or a cause helps make sense of what might otherwise be considered aberrant behavior. Knowing your spouse's unique history can help you overlook outbursts or bad habits that would otherwise be intolerable. Understanding something about what drives the deep devotion of a fan, a business executive, or a marginalized punk rocker, can help make sense of adult face painting, workdays that become work nights, and sneering at the status quo. By the same token, fallible men and women stick together because they know something about the other that helps make sense of the crazy things the other does.

True intimacy grows out of mature and tolerant understanding. Most reasonable people don't have to be reminded that no one is all that and a bag of chips. They know humans are limited creatures drawn together at points of weakness, not at points of strength. Privately, we know all too well about not measuring up at work, at school, at home, and in the bedroom. Clothes, makeup, bravado, and such are clever disguises that help keep secrets. *Can I truly trust you with my limitations, what I can't ever do or be? Can I be vulnerable with you?* The answer for lovers is *Yes!* Loving spouses are painfully aware that they hold the heart of one of God's favorite children. These couples commit to each other and communicate their dreams, heartaches, and vulnerabilities. They get it. What strengthens marriages is a keen appreciation and acceptance of our inabilities and limitations. "We," as one old song goes, "are weak, but he is strong."

If you've been married more than a week or two, you've already figured out that it's not a good idea to tell your spouse how she or he feels. As I've learned over the last half century in my own marriage, I don't fully understand. However, to keep peace, I better try. As I listen to Jodi talk about how she feels, I get a better—but still incomplete—understanding of what's going on inside her mind and heart. There are sound reasons why my understanding of her feelings are close but not entirely accurate.

The first is that her feelings, experiences, and reality are her personal possessions. Jodi's feelings, experiences, and reality were created inside her sack of skin in a place only she and God know. None of them exist outside of her. She takes in a variety of stimuli (sight, sound, touch, smell, etc.) and her brain then stitches all of it together into her customized version of what's happening. The result is influenced by variables that include, but are not limited to, time of day, place, actors involved, how she's feeling at the moment, and her past experiences and learning in similar situations. Like mine and yours, Jodi's take on reality, what's actually happening, is colored by her private interpretation. It belongs to her and is impossible to fully explain.

At the dawn of the twentieth century, Harvard's first psychologist, the pragmatist William James, suggested that what is apparent to one, may not necessarily be apparent to the other (2008/1899). That line was a startling revelation for the new disciples of psychology and explained why good teaching sometimes fails to connect. Just because the math teacher can factor a quadratic equation in her head and explain it aloud in detail does not mean the kids on the back row get it. Each kid in the class selects which of the millions of bits of information in the environment (how he feels, what he likes, the week's big game, who to ask to homecoming, and maybe something about equations) to process. From all of this, each kid puts together a personal understanding of quadratic equations. As evidenced by the next big math test, there will be a wide variety of understandings of equations, about as many as there are students in the class. The stark reality is that like you and Jodi and me, each kid will forever be alone with his or her understanding of the world.

While some of us may share bits and pieces of knowledge regarding education, politics, sports, and the best ice cream flavor, we will never completely understand the other. This tends to drive us into herds of *us* and *them*, in which we seek common ground with other like-minded folk; however, if we look deep enough, even on common ground there are divisions that can escalate into violence.

Most fighting on school playgrounds and in bedrooms is likely due to a lack of understanding and subsequent acceptance of differences. The inability or unwillingness to take the other's position, to see things as he or she does, is generally at the root of these skirmishes. Given that we can never fully understand our beloved, even feeble attempts at trying are effective in deescalating conflict.

Jodi has tried to tell me of the beauty and wonderment of classical music, but no combination of the twenty-six available letters can harness the same profound joy within me that classical music stirs in Jodi. Though we sit in the same concert hall and hear the same notes, she can be moved to tears while I nod off. She can tell me about her passion, but she cannot give it to me. Because I, too, have been powerfully moved by music (Leonard Cohen comes to mind), I can understand some of her passion, and that's enough to get us by.

We are all different. Emerson's great line, "Nature never rhymes her children, nor makes two men alike" holds a powerful truth. That beautiful set of words shapes our lives and affects the quality of our primary relationship with one of nature's other children. The reality of this poetic line—that we are ultimately alone—resonates with the soul in the darkest night when we are more susceptible to the truth; however, in the daylight of our senses, it seems too severe.

This immutable truth underscores the singularity of our existence and explains our longing for one another and our creator and exposes a foundational principle in our failure to understand the other. The unvarnished truth is that we never will achieve complete understanding. We must make peace with a partial understanding of our closest neighbor and our God. Our fingerprints and DNA have established that we are simply not cookie-cutter versions of one another. Each of us is a separate and single creation with a brain full of unique and unrepeated feelings, ideas, dreams, and experiences that no other human will ever fully know. Wisdom in human relationships begins with that reality. As Socrates ironically put it long ago, knowing that you do not know, is indeed to know. The pompous failure to accept that "for now, we see through the glass darkly" (I Corinthians 13:12) can rip apart fragile unions.

Each of us knows that we are alone in the very first and last instances of life. Secretly, I think we feel that's the case for all the days in-between, but that idea is too dark to entertain. We come into this world alone in a tiny bag of skin, and we leave in a larger, more wrinkled sack, full of experiences and stories of our own making. This bleak description of our time in an ill-fitting skin suit drives most of us to seek companionship. Few make it through life as loners. We need the comfort of a partner with whom we can be fully and imperfectly human.

True seekers know the unspeakable, internal void that even the most understanding human can't quite fill. The flashing signals from worlds beyond ours and the small daily miracles of respiration, sunlight, and timely kind words of strangers all testify that we are not alone. There is one who calls us into relationship that offers comfort beyond the capacity of a loving spouse. How and why the Creator reaches out and calls weak and heavy-laden people to rest in his embrace is the supreme mystery. To help us better understand, he used the human marriage model. Like that relationship, we don't fully understand the metaphor, but we can never take that gift for granted. Occasional glimpses of glory are the best we can manage for now.

Lovers Submit

Submitting is the element in the recipe that's really hard to swallow. It is also one of the most powerful secondary ingredients. Ironically it adds notes of sweetness and acts as a softening agent for hard-edged leaving and cleaving. For at least the last 2,000 years, we've viewed submitting as giving up or surrendering something precious we own, up to and including the self. Not to give away the punch line, but it is exactly that for men and women of faith. The willingness to submit in a relationship flows freely from a better understanding of who you are, who your partner is, and what's at stake.

According to its etymology roots, *submit* comes from the Middle English prefix *sub* (under or from below) and the Latin *mitte* (to send, as in submit a paper). Interestingly, the old Hebrew word (שִׁיעְגָּה) for *service* is the root of biblical *submitting*. Recently, this Christian verb and its derivatives have been used to signal weakness, rarely in a flattering manner. Consequently, including submission as a key ingredient for love making requires a bit of explanation and justification.

Some confusion may come from a cursory reading of Ephesians. In a quick glance at this familiar passage, it's easy to see why some interpret *submission* as a gender role, something the wife does. The often-cited reference (at least for men) is, "Wives, submit yourselves to your husbands" (Ephesians 5:22). Conveniently, we men tend to overlook the preceding and following verses. While some of us have heard Paul compare a man's love for his wife to the love Christ has for the Church, "that he gave himself for it" (Ephesians 5:25), few read the preamble to Paul's discussion of marital love. The key to understanding submission is tucked away in verse twenty-one. There, Paul writes of "submitting yourselves one to the other in the fear of God." As I read it, submitting is a two-way street that should be traveled frequently by loving husbands and wives alike.

You'll find this road untrodden if you rely on your instincts. The defense of self is a necessary, built-in, automatic protective mechanism that keeps us rocking and rolling. If you hear an unexpected loud noise, your eyes widen, your bronchial system expands, and blood rushes to your muscles, all in preparation for fight or flight. This autonomic response kicks in when you perceive a threat, real or imagined. Of course, most threats are harmless, but the stress on your body and relationships from repeatedly activating your body's warning system can be distressing. Dirty dishes, bad breath, sports, and Christmas travel plans are just a few silly issues that ignite this "protective" system with devastating results. While this system can't be turned off completely, it can be turned down. The key is understanding what's happening, who you are, and who you're defending yourself against. Knowing a little about the physiology of the body's automatic response might help, but most helpful is understanding yourself and your opponent.

Believers have an advantage in knowing themselves. They are ordinary human beings with no special powers, but they claim to know their manufacturer personally, and this Creator tells believers why they were created and how to flourish. His advice in times of conflict is to remember who you are and who you represent. The instruction manual he left advises, "When reviled, revile not again" (1 Peter 2:23), "Agree with thine adversary quickly" (Matthew 5:25), and "A soft answer turns away wrath" (Proverbs 15:1). In short, don't fight back, be wise and careful but "harmless as doves" (Matthew 10:16). For heaven's sake, don't waste your time defending yourself!

At the root of a lover's unwillingness to submit to the beloved may involve a twisted sense of pride, one of the biggest obstacles to a joyful life and happy marriage. On their best days, believers are able to swallow their pride and lay down their most precious possessions in deference to the beloved (see Galatians 6:3). The humility this selfless act demands is the essence of Christianity. What allows these ordinary men and women to defer to the other is a bone-deep understanding of Jesus's words, "Greater love hath no [husband or wife] than this, that [he or she] lay down [his or her] life (including restaurant preferences, paint colors, vacation plans, etc.) for [his or her] (best) friend" (John 15:13).

Submitting comes out of an understanding that the cruel angry words that rile us up come from weak and wounded people. In heated moments, stay strong. Write down poet Leo Rosten's great line, "I learned that it is the weak who are cruel, and that gentleness is to be expected only from the strong," and revisit it often. That insight sheds new light on conflict and changes our response. Seeing the situation through this compassionate lens changes things. With a better understanding of what's happening, leavers and cleavers serve (the old Hebrew translation of *submitting*) the conflict's casualties, especially those in their own households. The vows to love no matter what, to figuratively lay your life down for your spouse, test that resolve. However, this is not a license to abuse the other or stay in a dangerous relationship.

A lot of our sour opinions toward submission and reluctance to submit stem from our obsession with our own worth, especially compared to our neighbor's worth. Thinking you're better than everyone else may help grow your business or keep you atop the sporting world, but it's a lousy attitude in marriage. One big, flashing yellow light throughout Scripture is an inflated sense of self. Apostle Paul's warning against "thinking of ourselves more highly than we ought" (Romans 12:3) is an example. As the U.S. Constitution declares, it is self-evident that we are all created equal. Centuries before America's founding, Paul drove this point home, stating "there is no respect of persons with God" (Romans 2:11), including gender. Marriage is a two-vote proposition, and there must be submission from both sides for marital success over the long haul.

The good news is that we are already equal under the law, as there are no perfect men or women this side of the Pearly Gates. The hope we can all cling to is that God's amazing grace, like love, is boundless. God knows each of us from the inside out, and though he has our number, likes us anyway—warts and all. His demands for marriage candidates are simple: give all you have, including your life. As indicated in the Soul Owner's Manual, "Greater love hath no man than this, that he lay down his life for his friend" (John 15:13), a wake-up call for lax husbands and wives. This act of self-sacrifice, the essence of submission, is the epitome of love, a point speed-readers of the New Testament often miss.

Perhaps one reason the Bible is so often misread or misunderstood is that its instructions for loving God and loving others (Matthew 22:37–39) are written upside down and backward. Scriptural reasoning is often hard to follow and can appear contradictory. Essentially, the way to really live is to die, the way to have is to give away what you have, the way to be first is to be last, and the way up is down. To paraphrase Solomon, what seems reasonable and right may be unreasonable and wrong (Proverbs 14:12).

Seesengood (2019) pointed out that "Paul's central metaphor for Christian life and faith is slavery and servitude" (p.141-142). My wedding band symbolized that I unconditionally promised to love and serve Jodi with the same devotion that Christ loved and served the Church. In return, Jodi promised to love me, regardless. That wedding band reminds me and everybody else that I am captured by this woman. There is an unbelievable sense of freedom in being her prisoner. Whether you like me or not, I'm successful or a failure, sick or well, rich or poor, old or young, there's a gal at my house who promised to love me through it all. That gives me the freedom to do crazy things like write a book on love and marriage.

The old owner's manual also declares that if I want to be the head of my household, I best learn the ways of servanthood (Matthew 20:26–28). Jodi shouldn't follow me across the street if I'm not willing to wash her feet. In the same upside-down notion, my limitations as a human mean that I desperately need stuff like kindness, forgiveness, and understanding, and the way to get them is to give them away by the truckloads (Luke 6:38). If I'm at the end of my rope and I need to hang on, I need to let go (Philippians 4:6–7), and if I want to live my best life, I must die to self first (Matthew 16:25). The bond that joined Jodi and me was made from the residue of our connective tissue, ceremonially harvested at the marriage altar in 1971.

We knew that marriage was a serious promise, but in our haste didn't fully appreciate its demands and costs. The last five decades has shown us the price, giving us perspective we lacked on that hot August morning in 1971. Naively, we asked that an old Lebanese cleric's poem "On Love" be read at our ceremony. If we listened closely, Kahlil Gibran (1923/1998) would have given us a heads up on the price of "love's peace and love's pleasure." I include a portion of it here to alert you to what you're submitting to when you exchange some jewelry with that cute guy or gal.

> When love beckons to you, follow him,
> Though his ways are hard and steep.
> And when his wings enfold you yield to him,
> Though the sword hidden among his pinions may wound you.
> And when he speaks to you believe in him,
> Though his voice may shatter your dreams as the north wind lays waste the garden.
> For even as love crowns you so shall he crucify you. Even as he is for your growth so is he for your pruning.
> Even as he ascends to your height and caresses your tenderest branches that quiver in the sun,
> So shall he descend to your roots and shake them in their clinging to the earth.
> —*The Prophet,* Kahlil Gibran (1923/1998), p.11–15

The love that joins men and women is not to be trifled with. It is serious and demands that we learn the ways of "submitting ourselves one to the other" (Ephesian 5:21). Until couples are fully aware that "Even as love crowns you, so shall he crucify you," couples are not ready to be joined till death do them part. However, the courage and willingness to submit your dreams and aspirations and indeed your life to another has rewards beyond what can be imagined. Partnering with one who pledged to give his or her life for you, to serve you, makes negotiating life's hills and valleys a divine adventure. Holding hands through the valleys and sharing the breathtaking sights on the mountaintops are what you get when you give up your preferences for your spouse.

From Commitment to Submission and Back Again

The strange substance that binds the hearts of men and women may be better understood if we think about what we *do* to promote the warm mysterious feelings of connection—commit, communicate, understand, and submit. As these secondary ingredients blend, each contributing its unique flavor profile, the final whole becomes more than the sum of the parts.

As I hope you see, the order of ingredients matters. In the primary ingredients, leaving precedes cleaving, and poor leavers struggle as cleavers. The four secondary ingredients are intricately connected, each dependent on the previous and then pouring into the next as "way leads on to way," to borrow Frost's line. Following the model around and back again is particularly helpful in identifying problems and crafting solutions to the issues that compromise a human relationship.

To make a love that endures, you cannot cut corners or leave anything out of the recipe. Even if one or more ingredient is chronically weak, a marriage can fall apart. When the bond is broken, it's difficult, but not impossible, to fix. Interventions must be aimed at the cause, not the effect. Do this, and any problem that confronts husbands and wives can be overcome with additional commitment, clearer communication, fuller understanding, and an increase in Christ-like submission.

You may face incredibly sad times in loving another, but if the heart beats, there's hope. As sure as there are valleys on the EKG of a beating heart, peaks are always around the corner. There is promise of better days ahead for couples trekking through the mountains and the valleys of a loving relationship. Hope lies in the old recipe for a potent balm that can re-glue two broken hearts and, as Isaiah noted, make the crooked paths ahead a little straighter (Isaiah 45:2).

Identifying Problems and Solutions

If you deconstruct the old recipe for love, you'll identify some causes of and maybe prevent some potential heartaches ahead.

Couples in it for the long haul need a way to detect and fix weaknesses or breaches in the bonding agent uniting them. The model (Figure 1) is designed to help do just that. Clearly, love begins with a willingness to leave and cleave, but it is sustained with commitment, communication, understanding, and submission. Like the "begetting" sequence in the New Testament's opening chapter, one component seems to foster or beget the next. It appears the reverse is also true.

If you believe your problem is a commitment issue, look backward and see where commitment comes from. If this old recipe works, commitment is seeded in submission and bears fruit in communication. If you're unwilling to give the last full measure of love, "that he lay down his life for his (closest) friend" (John 15:13), expect some commitment issues. If the problem seems to be communication, the model suggests you might question your commitment. An unwillingness to stop what you're doing and pay close attention to the other may indicate a lack of commitment. Remember—if you're committed to a person or cause, you'll check in (communicate) regularly.

When it's clear that your partner isn't getting it and you suspect a problem in understanding, look backward at communication. Failing to understand is directly related to an inability to interpret the signals of communication that often come in code, without spoken words. Eye rolls and grins are just as important as the statement, "Pick up a gallon of milk on your way home." While you may never fully understand your spouse's devotion to Tennessee football, you get a sense of it when she nervously paces the living room floor as Alabama's Tide rolls into town. Learning to read facial expressions, tone of voice, body language, and the environment is critical to communication and understanding your honey's edginess, potentially saving you a heartache or two.

Sometimes your lack of understanding isn't your problem. When your spouse struggles with word choice, patience is critical. Feelings and emotions are hard to fit into words. Feelings of sadness are too big, weighty, and complex to fit inside S-A-D. Likewise, there are times when J-O-Y doesn't fit. The truth works in these cases. Admitting you don't understand is appropriate, because it is the truth. In these times, checking for understanding can pay off handsomely. Without judgment or bias, begin your sentence with, "So, what I think I hear you saying is . . ." This invites your partner's corrections, additions, or subtractions, thereby clarifying your partner's communication. This "pleasing sacrifice" is difficult to make, but helpful in straightening out garbled messages between two loving but separate souls.

Understanding also helps you avoid making mole hills out of mountains. Getting stuck in the decision-making process is common in two-vote marriages. How ties get resolved matters. Absent valiant attempts to understand the other's position, seemingly harmless issues quickly escalate. Typically, both parties go to their respective corners. When the bell sounds, they come out swinging, "protecting themselves at all times" as advised by human instinct.

Successful leavers and cleavers know that understanding is rooted in communication and flowers in submission. For these couples, when understanding is a problem, they immediately suspect a communication breakdown, and they fix it. If the two understand what's at stake in the fight, solutions and resolutions tend to emerge. This only happens in a safe environment for sharing raw feelings, emotions, and needs, but it requires the courage to talk and the sacrifice of listening, the essence of communication.

When you more clearly understand who you are (a limited being, capable of messing up regularly), who your partner is (for reasons still unknown, God's favorite child), and what's at stake (your family, the messy laboratory of Christianity), you are more prepared to submit. Giving up your preferences for the other becomes a natural, biblical response when you really get it. You'll even go to Applebee's when you proposed Red Lobster, because it's what lovers do.

It also works on the plus side. If you and your partner decide to work on your marriage and settle on communication as a place to start, it may help to look backward and renew your commitment to each other. Any improvements in communication result in a deeper understanding and appreciation of your partner, strengthening the bond between you. As an added bonus, choosing a restaurant on your next night out (likely a submission issue) will be easier and more fun.

It's a short step between submission and commitment, since it's easy to fully commit all that you are to people and causes for which you're willing to lay down your life. Going all in on a person or cause creates an urge to check in on that investment from time to time. You want to know more about the object of your obsession. The resulting communication helps build a more rounded understanding of that person and better explains why she's constantly late or he talks too much. These private insights about the beloved spread even more glue in the joints that bind you. The bedrock of understanding helps you overlook a snide remark about the restaurant you chose or put aside your agenda to go apple picking, especially during college football bowl season. The willingness to lay down your life for your spouse adds yet another layer of glue.

Completing the Unbroken Circle

Making love is complicated. If you're looking for concrete suggestions regarding where to start, remember that *love* is a verb. If you look close enough, each ingredient in love's recipe is also a verb, suggesting something to do or practice at home. For those who need a little help in the beginning, I attached some suggestions in the Appendix to get you started.

Sustaining a marital relationship built on love is a lifetime proposition. Inherent in that notion is the obligation to attend to the process. Love, like the people who make it, changes over time. It can blossom and mature with proper care and attention or decay if left unattended and unreplenished, dying of malnourishment. The list of threats—inattention, ungratefulness, and other rotten things ragged, imperfect human beings do to each other—outstretches love's list of ingredients. The opening sentence in Tolstoy's *Anna Karenina* says as much: "Happy families are all alike; every unhappy family is unhappy in its own way." It's a lot easier and more fun to be one of those "happy families."

Thankfully, the feelings I had for Jodi long ago have deepened to a more mature love. A half century ago, I thought I loved her, but those immature feelings have taken root, and I've feasted on its fruits for more than a half century. This brand of resilient love with an extraordinary adhesive power most often begins as a soft emotion, a thing, a noun. It is sustained by continual reaffirmation of things I must do to keep it relevant: commit, communicate, understand, and submit.

The precious primary and secondary ingredients in love are simple and ordinary, but they must be consciously chosen and freely selected. In their rawest form, each is a one-word description of a necessary action within a healthy and lasting marriage. Blending these ingredients creates a bonding agent that endures. If you and your partner are seriously considering making a fresh batch of the relationship glue, first consider the costs. If you decide to invest in all of love's ingredients, there is still work to do. The next section will try to explain what's left.

While expensive to make, I think you'll find that love, like a good pecan pie, is better when homemade.

Section V

NOTES ON COOKING UP A FRESH BATCH AT HOME

"If all else fails, read the instructions."

—My Wife, Jodi

Overview

Whether making a little banana bread on the sly, constructing a swing set, or cooking up plans for an amorous evening, you need basic materials, a pattern to follow, and some knowledge of the order of operations. Master chefs, mechanics, and old loving couples know the recipe by heart. They also instinctively know when important things are left out or ignored and the right tool to use and when to use it. Malcolm Gladwell in *Blink* describes the uncanny ability of these experienced old hands to detect flaws and fakes just by looking at the final product. They know when something's off just a little bit. To avoid that embarrassment, it would be helpful to revisit the old instruction book from time to time.

For beginners and those who feel "something's just not right," some simple how-to instructions are helpful, if not downright essential. The pictures from the previous chapter's model describe love's ingredients and how they relate to each other. In this section, I will describe what I've come to believe the final product ought to look like. Concrete instructions, as

I've painfully learned over the years, are important, at least for novices. I personally have a collection of nuts and bolts in my workshop left over from shaky beds and unstable furniture. To be fair, the bed and desk came with the "some assembly required" warning clearly labeled on the box. Over the years, I've tossed or ignored a lot of instructions, reasoning that someone with my advanced skill set wouldn't need them. Too often, we—especially those of us with a Y chromosome—fall into the trap of overestimating our knowhow or abilities. There's a good reason most of the trouble on a golf course comes short of the green. Golfers are notorious for thinking they can hit the ball farther than they actually can. In the kitchen and elsewhere, we can't be overconfident. And instructions matter.

With you in tow, I'll revisit the basics of the old recipe for homemade, married love and offer a few instructional notes dug out of my desk drawer that I finally pried open. I'll describe the utensils or tools any well-stocked kitchen needs. These include a heat source that transforms raw batter into cake and spices and improves the taste of dinner staples. I'll also let you in on a few secrets that make Jodi's cornbread and apple crisp the talk of Thanksgiving and Christmas dinners. Of course, after a sumptuous meal, somebody has to clean up. Believe it or not, that menial task is an act of love that I know from personal experience pays off handsomely.

As in almost any letter to friends, there are things I left out of the book and want to add, so the last chapter is my postscript. It includes insights that didn't fit into any of the previous chapters but may help clear up some things I said. For anyone who gets this far, I hope my ramblings spark your thinking and encourage you to add to my incomplete list of tips and tools that aid in structuring, nurturing, and maintaining an abiding love. Through your own trial and error learning, you will develop thoughts and advice on how marriage should work. Share your love stories with the folks around you. At the turn of the twentieth century, William James, America's first psychologist, opened up the new discipline of psychology and the old practice of education with a simple, penetrating line. He wrote, "What is apparent to one is not necessarily apparent to the other." It may be obvious to you why your love works but may not have ever occurred to the other. These hard-earned insights are invaluable, so share them. Don't be shy about telling anyone who will listen why and how your marriage works. After all, we are people of the "good news." Besides, we all have a clear and vested interest in better, more successful marriages. Our society is built on the bedrock of strong family life.

Chapter 16

WHAT IT TAKES TO MAKE LOVE AT HOME

[C]ooking done with care is an act of love.

—Craig Claiborne

THOUGH USEFUL IN GENERAL PRINCIPLES, metaphors, models, and analogies can be pushed beyond their usefulness, especially when they're mixed, and most especially when you use them to explain love. From the beautiful words of Solomon's Songs—"your eyes are doves," "your lips are scarlet threads," and "your cheeks are like halves of pomegranates" (1:15 and 4:3)—to Shakespeare's sonnet comparing his love to "a summer's day," we've all struggled to describe the indescribable. Love is impossible to fit into words. Consequently, this is not a book about blunt or sharp objects or the viscous properties of how to make and use Elmer's Glue. It is about what sticks two messy human beings together as they learn to peacefully coexist in a confined space and make the kind of ethereal love that feeds their souls and sees them through to payday.

Although not as poetic as Solomon's description and certainly more blue-collar, the old recipe and instructions for making married love in Genesis are clear. The frail and limited human body contains the raw material for the strong adhesive that knits hearts together, but the price tag scares most people off. We are asked to leave others, things, and comfortable traditions behind and cleave (glue ourselves) to another. From the beginning, we've had access to, but have rarely used, the expensive original tools to break down the human carcass and extract the additional secondary ingredients of love: commitment, communication, understanding, and submission. When stirred together with the two primary ingredients (leaving and cleaving) and allowed to simmer, the soft, subtle notes of joy, peace, patience, kindness, goodness, faithfulness, gentleness, and self-control arise and unify a relationship. These sweet fruits, as Paul described them in Galatians 5:22–23, sustain marriages over the long haul. Most old married folks will testify that the sacrifices demanded of lovers are well worth the costs, and more satisfying than any chef's dish.

Homemade Love: Yada, Yada, Yada

It's easy and wrongheaded to reduce love making to some form of sex. Longtime lovers know love is more than intercourse or sexual performance. It is deeper and more profound. It is an act of the will and not the fulfillment of an innate desire to copulate. There are undeniable times of tender physical intimacy in a relationship, but like sand, intimacy shifts with circumstance. As Matthew 7:24–27 points out, shifting sand is a poor foundation for permanent structures, especially marriage. Let me explain.

There are characteristics of human beings in tenth-grade biology books that distinguish men and women from lower forms of animals. Below is a beginner's list of nine things that help separate men and pigs (insert your own joke here).

Unlike pigs, men display the following:
- Erect posture
- Prehensile hands
- Forward vision
- Large, complex brain
- Complex voice mechanism
- Greater dependency in infancy
- Flexibility of innate drives (food, sex, etc.)

- Constant sex drive
- Longevity

Of course, there are obvious and important differences between a human being and the average pig. I know, because we raised a few pigs when I was a kid. Although the Poland China breed makes a good pork chop, they are poor playmates. They can't stand up, grip a baseball bat, judge distances, help you with your homework, or stay home if they find a hole in the fence. They expect to eat at a certain time every day, have babies well before their first birthday, and they don't hang around long enough to make friends.

Our best brood sow was old Brownie. She turned out about two to three litters of piglets a year. However, Brownie was not the romantic type, and I don't think she ever fell in love. Flowers and sweet talk didn't do it for her. Hormones did. There were signs that Brownie was in heat. The most obvious came during our early morning calls to get Brownie out of Mr. Potter's boar pen. Mr. Potter's old boar wasn't handsome and didn't smell good, but Brownie didn't mind. She was following a deeply embedded instinct that involved no thought as far as I could tell. When her biological clock went off, it was time, and she was ready. When she was not in heat, any pen would hold her, but nothing worked when she needed a boyfriend.

Humans are very different. They can do things Brownie could never do. The human sex drive is constant, and the slightest spark can ignite it. Although hormones are involved, they are more effect than cause. Circumstances or some amalgam of setting, confidence, feelings, health, and beliefs are common arsonists. It can happen in the cheap seats of an ice-cold stadium when he snuggles in for warmth, in the summer garden with sweat beading on her upper lip, at church when she's singing in the choir, early on a Tuesday morning getting ready for work, or Sunday night after church when you exchange "that look." In short, anytime, any place, anywhere. The potential for a sexual encounter is a constant we live with, and though dormant at times, the urge can easily be aroused when circumstances align.

Freud taught that sex is a constant and fundamental human need that will be satisfied one way or the other. It will either be sublimated, diverted, or modified into another form or activity that is more culturally or socially acceptable or be acted upon. Some masturbate or convert sexual energy and desires into the service of worthy causes, while others "hook up" in risky rendezvous with random partners. All find a way to satisfy this primal urge.

Marriage gives a safe, appropriate means to find satisfaction. The designer and outfitter of our clay frame anticipated that the original, intense method of begetting down through generations would be problematic. He proposed marriage as a reliable, steady outlet for his marvelous gift of sex. Interestingly, the old Hebrew word *yada*, translated as "know" was how Moses and the prophets talked about sex. It was the perfect way to describe an act that transcends intellectual understanding and infers a physical intimacy or complete union with another that may be expressed in sexual intercourse. Like many things, *yada* has been updated to fit our modern culture to mean "boring or predictable" or "empty words not worth repeating," as in "yada, yada, yada." The words in red in Matthew's gospel, though taken out of context, seem fitting: "It was not so from the beginning" (19:8).

Sex is all about *knowing* in its fullest sense—knowing the person, how things work, how to read signs and set conditions. The person you married is like you, a very real and messy person. So how can you better read the signs and set the conditions for intimate *knowing* with someone who is just as confused and confusing as you?

In my years of marriage counseling, my go-to sex speech goes something like this: "Get to know how the parts fit and figure it out." However, there are some things I should add, specifically the biological facts of which I was ignorant on my own wedding night. Here are a few things I've learned.

Having sex is not making love, at least the kind that holds two people together for a lifetime. It may be the result of commitment, communication, understanding, or submission. Of the four stages in the sexual response cycle—desire, excitement, orgasm, and resolution (Eisenberg, 2008)—orgasm is the briefest, most intense stage. At this height of sexual arousal the body involuntarily releases tension with extreme pleasure experienced in the genitals and throughout the body. Endorphins dump into the bloodstream and affect heart rate, blood pressure, breathing rate, and self-awareness. Exposed and vulnerable, you're accepted by the other in this tender moment and deeply cared for. Chasing orgasms measured only in seconds is a fool's errand. It is what happens before (desire and excitement) and after (resolution) that shape a marriage and set the conditions that ensure basic needs, including sex, are met.

Married or single, everyone knows something about the powerful allure of sex. Saints and sinners, preachers and teachers, moms and dads are all vulnerable. That's good news for married folks and a blinking caution light for those without a marriage license or who are temporarily apart from their spouse. In the right setting, this powerful primal urge can ignite the spark that saves a marriage; however, in the wrong circumstance, this same desire can set fire to the marriage contract.

We hold the reins to this powerful force raging in each of us. We can pull back and stop it (if it's not in full gallop) or loosen the reins and go for a ride. It's a choice we make, but there are consequences either way. None are immune to blatant sexual advances. Again, good news for wives and husbands at home and a red flag when they are apart. Stay vigilant on both counts. Remember that random acts of kindness might be Victoria's best kept secret, and for goodness's sake, when you leave your beloved at home, be wary of your human weaknesses.

We can't control everything, but there are many things we can. Each of us is wholly responsible and accountable for the words that come from our mouths and the things we do. How we talk to our spouse in the daylight affects what happens after dark. Vince Gill said it best in a song, "It's Hard to Kiss the Lips at Night That Chew Your Ass Out All Day Long." The old adage that the way a woman turns on a man is to walk into the room is cute, but not true. Believe it or not, it takes a bit more. Same goes for turning on women. Sometimes washing dishes is one of the sexiest things a man can do. It may not work, but it couldn't hurt. As a sign I saw declared, "No man has ever been shot by a woman while washing dishes." For men and women, sexual intimacy exposes our most vulnerable selves. Nourishing words and simple kindnesses throughout the day make the bedroom a safe place for both partners.

Making love may indeed involve orgasms, but it's deeper than that. What goes unsaid is that the new husband and wife are fully expected and licensed to make the love that will keep them bound to each other for a lifetime. The glue that holds them together is more than physical intimacy. It consists of constant vigilance, upkeep, and a willingness to make a fresh batch now and then. Love made on the honeymoon is magical and amazing, but it can quickly fade in the daylight of reality. It might need replenishing when the newlyweds get home and are confronted with jobs, new routines, and unexpected responsibilities. Intimacy can fix many things, but the sex act is only a fraction of the love made at home, and most is done fully clothed. It is each spouse's responsibility to keep an eye on the love supply and churn out a new batch when needed.

Toward that end, the old recipe I offered has fed love-starved humans since Eve made an honest man of Adam. After examining the old words for *love* and listening to countless couples whose supply was exhausted, I propose a handful of ingredients for your love pot. As with any recipe, it must be salted and spiced to taste, but I'm convinced that these four ingredients are the foundation of the hearty stock that gives love its sweet aromas and sticking power.

Like the sloppy word *love* we toss around to describe how we feel about biscuits and gravy and our newborn grandchild, we rarely contemplate the meanings and obligations in commitment, communication, understanding, and submission. Maybe because each gets regular airplay in everyday language, no further explanation is necessary—everybody knows what they mean. I disagree. Of all people, serious lovers looking for lifelong partners need to become better acquainted with the challenges, risks, and rewards of these four powerful ingredients in love making.

All the folks this side of the Pearly Gates have a well-earned reputation for messing stuff up, especially good things. To paraphrase the Apostle Paul, the stuff I should do I can't seem to find time for, but somehow I find lots of time for things I shouldn't do (Romans 7:19). The bad news is that the marriage ceremony does not magically transform either party (for example, see Jodi and me and our children). We all blow it every now and then.

Though it usually takes place at the altar, the marriage ceremony doesn't redeem the soul or rewire the parts of our personality not subject to the will. The good news is that love can change a lot of bad human behavior, including what Apostle Peter labeled "a multitude of sins" (I Peter 4:8). I know of no relationship issue that can't be fixed by reinforcing one of love's primary or secondary ingredients. I also am aware that a relationship missing any one of them will not endure. Consequently, there is a role for each of these ingredients in the love pot.

Those familiar with what goes on in the kitchen know that assembling the ingredients is just the beginning. To whip up a Denver omelet, there are steps after cracking a few eggs. You must locate a hunk of cheese, a couple of jalapenos, and some ham, then these ingredients must be processed, mixed, and cooked. To do that, you need a few kitchen tools and a heat source, then you need some spices before you serve it up. That's not unlike the process of making glue that holds human beings together. Here are a few things you might need.

The Right Utensils

William, an old friend, grew up on grits and eggs, fresh corn, fried chicken, biscuits, and gallons of sweet tea. We all did in South Georgia. When I went off to college and he joined the military, we lost touch for a while. After a decade in the K-12 classroom, I changed lanes and helped prepare teachers at the collegiate level. One semester William showed up unannounced on the front row in my Educational Psychology class. Catching up after class, I learned that the military trained William as a chef, and he could now make a variety of impressive-sounding meals like chicken cordon bleu, bananas flambe, and other dishes I can't pronounce and neither of us grew up eating. He saw I was impressed and insisted on coming to my house and cooking for Jodi and me.

That evening, William showed up with a long wooden toolbox full of knives, spatulas, and other strange cooking utensils. He wore a spiffy white outfit and a tall chef's hat, which I learned had a fold for every way he could cook an egg. In William's hands, the sharp knives made a kind of hissing sound as he made short work of cutting up chicken and preparing a fresh vegetable side dish. He seemed to have a special knife for each task, and it was a joy to watch this professional work. Needless to say, I was impressed. The meal was even better than advertised.

Tools matter. Abraham Maslow reportedly said, "If the only tool you have is a hammer, you tend to treat everything like a nail." Hammers are wonderful tools, and they deserve a prominent place in the well-prepared carpenter's toolbox. However, if you're breaking down a chicken or installing a fragile glass pane, a good claw hammer may not be your tool of choice.

Learning when and how to use the right tool is transformative, but it takes time. Even with William's extraordinary toolbox, I would be lost if I had to make any kind of chicken dish. I need a clear, easy-to-follow recipe and basic tools. There are knives and then there are *knives*. A single knife, like the one William wielded in my kitchen, would set you back about $200—if you could catch it on sale. However, you can get a free set of knives for opening a savings account at your local credit union. Expensive tools can make cooking a lot easier, but you don't have to spend a day's pay for the cheap ones. For cooks like me, a free steak knife works. Archaeologists have discovered that our hungry ancient ancestors knapped rocks to butcher woolly mammoths.

Basic tools that help prepare primary and secondary ingredients for love's stew pot include a rock-hard willingness to leave, the daring to cleave, a commitment to endure, a promise to communicate, the patience to understand, and the raw courage to lay down your life. But you don't need to chip rocks or enroll in the credit union to get these effective tools. Like the tools in William's fancy toolbox, they're available to even the most inexperienced cooks. There is, however, some bad news. These tools with which you can make a lifetime's supply of homemade love will cost you more than a day's pay. They demand a full and complete surrender of your life at the marriage altar. But don't worry. They have an amazing return on investment.

A Good Heat Source

It might be helpful to refresh our collective knowledge on the cooking process. I'm certainly no kitchen expert, as you may have deduced from my banana-bread experience. I've never sat in a Home Economics class or tried out my sister's Easy Bake Oven. However, I have consumed a lot of good and bad food over the years, and I can read. Here's what I have learned about cooking.

First, make sure you have the right ingredients. If you're going to boil an egg or make a pan of banana bread or bake chocolate chip cookies, start with fresh eggs and know the difference between baking powder and powdered sugar. Ingredients matter, because raw eggs aren't as tasty as raw cookie dough. To make eggs and dough a little tastier, there must be a physical and chemical change in the internal structure of the egg and a way to get the flour, sugar, and soda to mix at the molecular level.

The thing that gets molecules excited and motivated to interact is a temperature change. On the Alaskan tundra a heard of musk ox, like molecules, huddle in tight wads, contracting together when the temperature drops. In the summertime, they spread out and expand. That same principle happens with eggs, dough, wooden boards on the back deck, and human beings. Things get bigger when the heat turns up and smaller as things cool down.

The heat that makes the magic happen in the kitchen, fire pit, or bedroom, is a function of temperature and motion, which together is a way to describe energy. All matter—everything we can see, touch, taste, or feel—is made of tiny atoms, each with electrons orbiting its core. Things, including people, that appear perfectly still, cold, or indifferent are churning on the inside, with more activity than any of us can imagine.

Atoms, God's tiny Lego set, make up all that is, but they are impossible to see with the naked eye. Although you can't detect it, electrons circling atoms in a lump of coal, scraps from an old building project, and your new phone's cardboard box are always moving. Even in a cold fish, there is heat. If you can transfer enough heat to the coal, scraps in the fireplace, cardboard box, or cold fish, you can rearrange their atoms. As you learned in seventh-grade science, matter—a.k.a. stuff—can be neither created nor destroyed. It may appear that you get rid of trash by burning it, but all you do is change its shape from a solid to a gas. However, if you're industrious, you can have a pretty satisfying fish dinner that will become fuel that turns up your internal thermostat.

If the metaphor holds, heat that transforms and shapes our world and relationships is ever present in everything and everybody. It has been there all along. We're tasked with figuring out which knobs control the temperature and how hot is too hot. A pork chop can be burned or undercooked, and both are unfit to eat. If the bedroom is too hot or too cold, nobody gets any rest. Guidance from Scripture suggests giving latitude in figuring out the thermostat setting that works for both. "Marriage," the Hebrews writer declared, "is honorable in all, and the bed undefiled" (13:4). Part of the fun is discovering the Goldilocks Zone in which each partner is comfortable.

The behavioral model introduced earlier can guide this exploration. It suggests problems and their solutions in a relationship are a function of commitment, communication, understanding, and/or submission. Everything from sex to budget problems can find their roots in commitment, communication, understanding, or submission. Like any marital problem, resolving these issues should be guided by each partner laying down his or her life for the other. With that caveat, boundaries in sex, spending habits, and thermostatic settings can be amicably negotiated and renegotiated if circumstances change. When imperfect, ragged, needy people trade hearts at the altar, their union is a continuing exercise in problem-solving. Should you be one of those altar-bound hopefuls, take heart. You get to engage in this lifelong exercise with one of God's favorite children.

Spice to Taste

Those who spend a little time in the kitchen know that homemade mac and cheese is more complicated than opening a box of elbow macaroni and pouring it over a block of Velveeta. Secondary ingredients and process matter. These secondary ingredients may not garner mention in the title of the dish, but they're vital. They prepare the two stars to work together and tease out the best in these two primary ingredients, introducing flavors and textures that are different and tastier than either primary ingredient boasts in its raw state.

To make the dish more personal, cooks fiddle with cheeses and combinations, experiment with different kinds of macaroni, and add meats (bacon, chicken, lobster, etc.), truffles, peppers, garlic, and even pumpkins. They bake it, boil it, or fry it. Whatever extra ingredient gets added and however the process varies, each dish includes the two stars of the show: macaroni (pasta) and cheese.

Like mac and cheese, love can be personalized, but you must know and respect the basics. Remember, love includes a willingness of both marriage candidates to leave everything and cleave to the beloved. Like a good macaroni and a quality cheese, leaving and cleaving must be cultivated over time and processed correctly. If you're wondering how, here's a pro tip: Do the verb. Leave and cleave as if your life depends on it. If you're still confused, stir into the mix appropriate measures of commitment, communication, understanding, and submission.

We easily forget that the squiggly lines on the back side of our fingers indicate where the Creator signed his art pieces—each, a beautifully uneven and flawed masterpiece. These flesh-and-blood works of art are commissioned to walk off the artist's bench and independently choose their life's path and deal with the consequences that come from that path. To no one's surprise, these individually crafted human art pieces, made from the dust of the earth, make countless choices—good and bad—on their long march to eternity. These choices include selecting traveling companions along the way. Like every decision, choices of a mate come with consequences, most which are enjoyable and some are unanticipated, but all must be lived out.

It should come as no surprise that messy humans make shortsighted judgments on a regular basis that can lead to troubled relationships and marriages. These slipups are difficult to fix after the fact, but not impossible. Fortunately, Scripture makes redemption the central theme of the gospel. The verb *love* is a consequential choice we may reject or affirm daily. Yesterday's mistakes can be corrected, and love can be restored by sound choices today.

That said, bad choices create problems that must be addressed. The stench of yesterday's poor choices can either serve as a reason to sever ties that bind couples or to engage in relationship-strengthening problem-solving. The most popular and ineffective strategy is to ignore a significant marital issue and treat it as if it never existed. Couples hope the problem goes away or slips off into the night. However, even the darkest night is followed by the rising sun, bringing the old problem into the light with each new day. Of course, there are other equally unproductive ways to handle problems that provoke marital discord. The only proper response is change. There must be a difference made in the people involved, the situation, circumstances, or the setting. Most of us know that, but we don't know how to get started.

There is little to no accounting for why, but heat preferences run the gamut from bland to four-alarm fire. I've been to enough Thai restaurants to know that what I consider spicy is judged tasteless for the guy at the next table. Jodi and I have been married so long that we're now on our third bottle of Tabasco. Given the previous discussion on limits, what's hot and what's not, I encourage you to explore the possibilities with the only limits imposed by love.

Marriages, problems, and solutions are all different, individually shaped by the tastes of those involved. No two people are exactly alike. Fingerprints, DNA codes, and toothbrushes are not shared. When two unique individuals decide to "forsake all others" and "cleave only to this one," the union they form is the only one like it in the world. Your siblings' marriages will look, feel, and be different, even though you share parents and some DNA.

Over the years, Jodi and I have resolved hosts of issues, and our solutions were based on who we are as individuals. What worked for Jodi and me may not be effective for you and yours. Besides, like the quart of milk in our fridge, each solution has an expiration date that shouldn't be ignored.

Frank discussions and disagreements forced us to pay attention to our individual tastes and preferences and cobble together a collective pattern that suits both of us. My preference of smoked oysters on salad and a drop of Tabasco on fried eggs are very different from Jodi's. However, over years of trial-and-error experimentation, we have adapted, with the possible exception of the baloney omelet with curry I served to Jodi—well, once. After fifty-three years, we've figured out most of the big stuff, like where to spend Thanksgiving and Christmas and the spice levels the other prefers.

It takes a while to settle on how your partner likes eggs and the kind of spices to keep on hand to make dinner "just right." For most of us, the spice options are simple—salt and pepper. However, these are just two of many choices that can transform an ordinary bowl of turnip greens into something special. As a matter of fact, I've discovered more than 500 other herbs and spices that nature offers to create endless combinations of flavor profiles that appeal to at least some of us.

Like the broad categories of cultural heritage (Asian, Caucasian, African, Hispanic, Indigenous, etc.), spices are unevenly grouped according to certain flavor characteristics—sweet, savory, sour, salty, and bitter. Too much of this or too little of that can be a real problem at the dinner table. Most lovers' spats begin as simple misunderstandings or issues of taste. These unforced errors begin as hairline fractures in commitment, communication, understanding, or submission.

Ironically, the fix likely comes from the same category in which the issue bubbles up. A misunderstanding or conversation that goes sideways can usually be patched up with a clearer signal of wants, needs, or desires. In short, better communication. Over the years, Jodi and I have learned to stay vigilant and not let things get out of hand. It's much easier to fix little things that are hard to detect but easy to cure.

Like a bowl of unseasoned turnip greens or unsalted fried eggs, the marriage relationship can be so unsavory that we lose our appetite for the things that sustain us. With the addition of a pinch of the right spice, a bland date night can be upgraded to *Wow!* status (see Appendix for specific ideas). I am not advocating a wild, exotic, spicy dish for every meal, but a little Tabasco on occasion can make breakfast something special.

Experimenting with new ways of spicing up food or relationships demands uncommon levels of courage and effort. But keep in mind, the individual nature of marriage is uncommon as well. Whoever thought we'd see TV ads for Spam with the tag line, "Don't knock it till you've fried it"? Like so many things in a human relationship, the hard work of learning the preferences and tastes of your partner and weaving them into your life together takes commitment, communication, understanding, and submission.

The Dishes Must Be Washed

On Thanksgiving, we host a big meal with neighbors, friends, and family, about twenty-five people total. The cooking chores are spread among our guests. Norman and Judy bring fancy green beans, and Bill and Lynn bring a fresh salad that would make Martha Stewart jealous. Zach and Loes provide a succulent roasted turkey and carve the meat. Matt and Andi bake pies and smoke the meat he harvested, while Karl and Susan set out a show-stopping sweet potato casserole and a selection of other sweets. Jodi and I fill in the menu blanks, including that good cranberry sauce that makes a sucking sound as it slides out of the can. Of course, Jodi also makes at least two pans of her famous jalapeno cornbread dressing.

Guests begin arriving around three o'clock with arms full of gorgeous, delicious food plated on fine china. To the untrained eye, every dish appears as if it were always precisely cut and ordered and ready to serve. That's not the case. Like our guests, I fawn over Jodi's beautiful pan of jalapeno dressing, but its finished beauty obscures the preparation mess it creates in our kitchen. Boiling, peeling, and dicing eggs; chopping celery and onions; mixing cornbread; processing the jalapenos; and putting it all together leaves a trail of dirty dishes to be cleaned up before company arrives. As the sous chef, that leaves me with dishes to wash, and most dishes get washed more than once. I suspect every home that produces these exceptional dishes has someone on KP duty.

When we finally gather in a big circle, we grab a hand and count our blessings. Then dinner is served at one of three tables in our living room and kitchen. After dinner and a rich dessert or two, we visit and play games. Usually there's a card game at one table, Trivial Pursuit at another, and dominoes or rummy at the third. At all three tables, scores don't matter. The games just give us something to do as we catch up on lives and loves and listen to Norman's jokes we haven't heard in a year. By about eight o'clock, the tryptophan begins to take effect, and slowly the guests drift away with to-go boxes and hugs. The conversations and sense of belonging the evening generates are as nourishing and satisfying as the elaborate meal, unless you count Andi's pecan pie.

If you think this sounds like great fun, you're right. But I confess it makes me a little tired. Because each of those once-a-year treats are served on dishes and prepared in pots and pans that have to be washed before they're sent home. This is complicated as we only have one dishwasher that must be plugged in, and it quickly fills with twenty-five plates, glasses, and silverware sets from dinner. Since I have limited culinary skills, my job usually includes scraping gravy and mashed potatoes out of the pots and pans, and with Loraine's help, handwashing a steady stream of utensils and cookware that made the evening possible.

In order for the marital bond to thrive, love must be served up much more often than once a year. A quiet old cowboy's wife asked him why he never said, "I love you." He slowly turned and said, "I told you thirty years ago when we married, and nothing ain't changed." Don't be the quiet old cowboy. The relationship between human beings is a living thing that must be fed a balanced diet regularly. Like a fine meal that feeds the body and soul, a marital relationship takes a lot of behind-the-scenes work to make a fresh dish of homemade marital love. It takes work to prepare and involves simple menial tasks, such as chopping onions, peeling boiled eggs, mixing it all up, and cleaning up the mess it leaves behind. But I suspect loving couples know how sexy washing dishes might be. Here is a quick list of other simple aphrodisiacs that create an ambiance that nurtures the sweet things that keep relationships alive (more complete ideas are offered in the next chapter).

- Wash the dishes
- Say "I love you" often
- Listen
- Make time for your spouse

- Throw a surprise party
- Clean up (inside and out)
- Be kind
- Forgive
- Be optimistic
- Be patient

Chapter 17

FINAL THOUGHTS, ADDITIONAL SPICES, AND FREE ADVICE ON LEAVING AND CLEAVING

Finally, brothers and sisters, whatever is true, whatever is noble, whatever is right, whatever is pure, whatever is lovely, whatever is admirable—if anything is excellent or praiseworthy—think about such things.

—Philippians 4:8

IN THIS CHAPTER YOU'LL FIND homemade advice that might be of use in helping personalize your recipe. These observations are rooted in my understanding of the fundamental Scriptural admonitions to love God and love our neighbor (especially our closest one). I have taken the liberty to propose how these two laws, which are at the heart of Christian commitment, might work in real life. My opinions have been further shaped and colored by my perceptions, biases, and experiences. To understand why and how, read the third chapter of Philippians (especially verses 12–14) before you get any deeper into my personal take on how things ought to work.

Like the Apostle who left us that raw truth, I am fully aware that I've not yet arrived at anything approaching perfection, and my less-than-perfect condition seeps into all I say or do. However limited by our inability we may be, there is no reason to quit trying. Like the Apostle, we are all pressing toward that impossibly high mark of perfection, but we're still a long way out. So don't be disappointed when you spot holes in my thinking. Instead, take my ragged thoughts, strain them through your understanding, and see if they fit. The ones that do, make them your own. Ignore the rest. Like the Apostle and me, you are working out your own salvation (Philippians 2:12) and your own marriage.

After slogging through a mountain of nouns and verbs that describe my limited take on the biblical how-tos of holy matrimony, you deserve a personalized prescription for your marriage. It's right to wonder how you can improve your marriage, and the answer should be individually tailored to you, your spouse, and your circumstances. While that is impossible in a general text, I can offer some homemade solutions I've found useful that serve as a good place to start your search for a way forward. From there, I suggest you find a pastor, counselor, friend, or fencepost and pour your heart out. For some, it's helpful to just get the poison out of your system, all those things you can't say out loud. For others, it may take a while and require the assistance of a professional guide to find your way out of the woods. Be patient, practice perseverance, and look for the good. Together, these three qualities are what Angela Duckworth called *grit*, a learnable human attribute that's more potent in success than intelligence, personality, ability, or status (Duckworth, 2016). Those with grit tend to live out their commitments and finish the race.

The following ideas are just that, ideas. They are my gritty suggestions to do something good for your closest neighbor, the one you're obligated to love. While some suggestions may sound strange, even backward, that's a biblical pattern we noticed previously. The way to live is to die, the way to lead is to serve, the way to be free is to get captured, and the way to get what you need is to give that away. So, advice based on these old notions may indeed sound funny, but I can report that they work. In my life, these bits of advice have strengthened the chords that bind Jodi and me and repaired some that frayed in the heat of battle.

I can also testify that these ideas will demand an uncommon measure of grace that's available to us all. But ideas and advice aren't magic. They must be acted on, tried out in the real world where some things work sometimes and for some people. I've included them here as part of the smorgasbord of choices to build your plan and get even better at loving another. Take what you need, but need what you take.

Plans and the ideas that undergird them are useless on the page. As effective plant managers and teachers know, plans don't work. People do. If you can't get real, imperfect, ragged human beings to do things, even the best plans are useless. As former heavyweight champ Mike Tyson said, "Everybody has a plan until they get punched in the mouth." Unless you can find a way to make these ideas work for you, they're just a collection of words worth very little. As I understand the Scriptures, why we do things matters most in affairs of the heart. For heaven's sake, follow its lead. A better marriage may be one step away.

Now, to my suggestions.

Write love notes. When I taught seventh grade math, I usually started class with a gag or joke to relax them (and me) before tackling the serious things like simple probability theory. Here's an example.

Three men are walking down the street. Two of them walk into a bar. The third one ducks.

If you have a driver's license, you probably rolled your eyes, but it would have killed with my seventh graders. Why they laugh or what makes jokes fun is the surprise at the end. Unexpected, positive surprises release dopamine in our brains and generate pleasurable feelings. Even the smallest gesture of genuine kindness can break the monotony of the ordinary, capturing attention and generating a sense of excitement, anticipation, and curiosity. If you are a teacher or want to make your beloved's day, this is useful insight. I wouldn't suggest telling my joke, but it would be a capital idea to leave a surprise love note in your spouse's sock drawer or a bad homemade poem under the stack of pillows on your bed. Like my joke, it's not the quality of the note that matters, but it's the thought that counts. Unexpected personal love notes nurture the joy that sustain you in rough patches that probability theory suggests are coming your way.

Let go and hang on. This is the bumper sticker for leavers and cleavers. Simply put, love asks you to be willing and courageous enough to let go of old ways and hang on to your beloved through thick and thin. How-tos are embedded in the backward logic of Scripture, as the way to let go is to hang on and the way to hang on is to let go. What that means in practical terms is determination to cling to your partner. I bet you can come up with things to let go of, and other things to hang on to for dear life.

Show up and shut up. Do this when the other is struggling to make sense of loss, disappointment, and despair. There are times when words are inappropriate or don't fit. Sometimes things don't work out. Even the best of us gets sick or dies, loses a job, gets divorced, and does rotten things. Inevitably, friends at funerals, hospital bed sides, and in divorce court offer a kind, loving thought that translates, "I know exactly how you feel. I, too, lost my mom, had a cancer diagnosis, or had a brother who (fill in the blank)." While pardonable and understandable, the one who's hurting knows what the well-meaning friend says isn't true. That friend can never know the depth of someone else's loss, sorrow, disappointment, or loneliness. If you truly want to be an instrument of God's peace in these terrible times, do these two uncommon, powerful actions: Show up and shut up. *Nothing* is most often the best thing you can say. Your warm embrace or simple touch is a lot more eloquent than any worn out phrase you can think up. Your stillness provides the hurting one an opportunity to talk, to get the strings of rotting sentences out of his or her gut. Once the other has an opportunity to speak the unspeakable, to clarify her or his feelings, to put disappointment into an understandable sentence, only then may your stories be appropriate. But maybe not. If in doubt, stay quiet.

Use a study guide. Scripture warns, "do not think of yourself more highly than you ought" (Romans 12:3). Marriage is a partnership of imperfect equals. One way to spin this dismal reality is to recognize the room for growth as you strive to measure up to love's high bar. High-stakes tests measure how much you must grow to meet the standards in medicine, law, teaching, Spanish, and third grade. In effect, students are measured against what people in that category or class must do to move on. For instance, medical students ought to be able to distinguish between viral and bacterial infections and Spanish I students should be able to conjugate common Spanish verbs.

As it turns out, there is an old marriage exam that has been extensively field-tested over two millennia. An impressive array of data on its reliability and validity evidence attest to its soundness as an indicator of one's love quotient (LQ). If you want to take a crack at it, flip to I Corinthians 13:4–8, home to what is commonly called "the love chapter." Your LQ indicates your readiness to love unconditionally by specifying the standard characteristics expected in lovers.

The I Corinthians 13 chapter is a study guide for the final exam we all take on loving one another. It's intended to help you evaluate where you are on the scale and what kind of work you need to do to prepare. If you have a fragile ego, this may be a little rough. Most of us do miserably on pretests, but that's expected on this side of the Jordan. That's okay. While we have lots of room for improvement, we have the rest of our lives to practice. While you still have time, study up on love's ways (I Corinthians 13) to understand this is not about you and your righteousness. You will always mess stuff up, but someone else will promise to love you anyway. That is the miracle of marriage and the good news of the Gospel. When the final bell rings and "study hall" ends, everything rides on your final exam, which covers your knowledge of love and what you've done about it. I hope you pass. If you ride on Jesus's coattails, you certainly will.

'Fess up and make up. After getting terrible results on the practice test above, you may be down in the dumps. Cheer up! If you're engaged or married or breathing, somebody loves you despite your faults. It may come as a surprise, but your inadequacies are not unknown to your beloved. Here is an activity and some advice that could help you understand this issue and how love "covers a multitude of sin" (I Peter 4:8): confess your sins (James 5:16). Word on the street is that it's a healthy thing to do.

Here's how. You and your partner sit down and write out five characteristics that make you a poor choice as a marriage partner. Then read your list to one another without comment. It might be a good idea to hold hands during this confession. When you finish, ask your partner if anything on your list is breaking news to him or her, and discuss.

When you made a mental list of desirable characteristics in a marriage partner, I'm guessing the items on your partner's "confession list" were not included. You never dreamed of marrying a self-centered boy or a girl who complained too much. But you chose this one, and you probably already knew he was "too selfish" or she "complained too much." The big question is why?

Now list at least five characteristics of your beloved that outshine his or her abrasive behavior, tendencies, and flaws, and why you chose that imperfect person as your life partner. When you both finish, read your lists. Now, each of you choose something in both lists to improve on, strengthen, or eliminate.

Be the partner you need. By now, you've figured out that we are all deeply flawed, needy creatures. When you're frustrated, flummoxed, and fuming at or with your lover, it seems clear that if he or she just did _____, your life would be so much better. The clouds would part and the birds would sing again. But how do you get your spouse to be the answer for you and your needs? A big confrontation can work—if a sufficient power differential is maintained. The problem is that when power is used exclusively to resolve human conflict, it tends to corrupt the very thing it intends to fix. There must be a better way.

My suggestion for thoughtful leavers and cleavers is to take a dose of the prescription I found in Luke 6:19. It has healed breaches and repaired holes in human hearts and relationships for centuries. Though effective and producing generally positive side effects, it's as awful to get down as castor oil. The prescription works like this.

List three things you need from your partner that would make your life better, easier, or more enjoyable and might resolve the conflict. If you're having trouble thinking of specific things, use the list in Galatians 5:22–23. Those items have helped resolve all kinds of human issues. They include love, joy, peace, patience, kindness, goodness, and gentleness as starters.

Now that you have a list of specific things you need, take the medicine that cures your ills and amazingly gets others to give you what you need. That is of course, if you are man or woman enough to take it. The prescription in Luke 6:38 demands that whatever you need, you give it away, and others will then give it back in heaps and piles. The distasteful part is that if you need to be listened to, listen to your partner. If you need to be more respected, give respect to those from whom you need it. If you desperately need attention, pay more attention to the other. If you need friends, be friendly. That's hard medicine to take, but it works!

Try it out in the lab first. A big part of why some marriages work is the fruit of the Spirit they feed on. As healthy and pure as words like *love*, *kindness*, and *gentleness* are, figuring out what their active ingredients are and what they mean to a relationship is messy business. Through trial and error, happy couples discover what long-suffering and goodness look like and when and how they can help. Most couples know what to say and what behavior pushes the wrong button, but in most loving relationships, situations can be misread. Words that worked last week are, to be kind, ineffective. Knowing when to speak or stay quiet provides eureka moments that offer valuable insights for couples who want to build a stronger union. There is always some fine tuning and adjustments to be made, but we don't always know which direction to turn the dial. Curious lovers continually tinker with what works and what doesn't. Knowingly or not, we generalize learning from these untidy matrimonial experiments to the wider world. The glue that holds a society together is first tested in covenanted relationships. Consequently, if you think society needs more kindness and gentleness, try it out at home. Then field test what you've learned at the ballpark, the mall, and in the parking lot. If it's as effective as advertised, go global with your discovery. Remember, the family is the laboratory for the Spirit-filled life and growing its fruits.

Leave a family legacy. I've seen parents hover over their children and swoop down to deliver what they think the child needs. Moms and dads, often at the expense of their relationships, sell out to give their child the latest iPhone, coolest clothes, and other things that won't last. As a graduate professor, I've had young men and women sit in my office and tearfully talk about their broken homes and the pain it has caused. With few exceptions, they rarely complain about what they don't have that takes a credit card to buy. It seems the most lasting and impressive gift a husband and wife can leave their children is an example of two fallible people showing their children that the promises of love last through good times and bad. That example endures through the ages and is a solid foundation on which to build a life. Having that permanent touchstone is more precious and expensive than a pair of Gucci loafers and will certainly last longer. A car, a down payment on a house, or even a college education are fine if you can afford them. But none of them are worth sacrificing a relationship with your children or spouse. When they leave your house after graduation, you want your children to say with confidence, "My momma loved my daddy, and my daddy loved my momma." That legacy is the rarest of gifts.

Remember little things mean a knot. The wisest, saddest man who ever lived warned that "little foxes spoil the vine" (Song of Solomon 2:15). He is explaining that people in a committed relationship should pay attention to the nitpicky stuff that irritates their partner. Likewise, you should keep an eye on early warning signals from your beloved that something might be wrong. Not washing a dish, throwing your socks on the floor, or chewing with your mouth open may not show up on your radar, but if it offends your closest neighbor, it's a problem. My own cautionary tale might save you some heartache.

I once had a cute little VW bug. On the way home, I noticed a strange sound from the engine in the back. Not being a very good mechanic, I ignored it. After all, the car was still running. The noise persisted, and I did the only thing I knew to do. I turned up the radio volume loud enough to cover up the noise. A few miles down the road, the noise got louder and eventually, the car left me by the road, alone in the dark. I had to get professional help to get my dead Bug off the highway and me back home. Had I been more diligent and attentive, a cheap, easy fix could have quieted my engine and saved my Bug's life. The knot in my gut that evening was caused by my negligence. For the price of a quart of oil I lost something I loved.

Don't just do something, stand there. We Americans created a can-do nation. We want to help, to lend a hand. While that's noble and proper in most situations, it's not always the best policy. Fortunes have been made and lost and military men and women have shed blood because of knee-jerk reactions to get in the fray and do something, anything to help. Sometimes we need to be still, to stand back and watch, to be present. As indicated in the tip to show up and shut up, silence and stillness are more important than charging headlong in a situation you don't know much about.

Although impulsiveness may cause more problems than it solves, the real tragedy is that we miss the beauty, power, and glory all around us. Moments of awe and wonderment are necessary in our busy lives, but we're too often driven by the latest trends on our social media feeds. As an old Sierra Leonean once told me, "The difference between Americans and Africans is that Americans spend time while Africans take time."

I've heard church friends say, "I would love to see a miracle," while overlooking the miracle of having a mouth that can form the word *miracle*. Their problem is that miracles aren't in a handheld device. They happen every day, but you have to "be still" (Psalms 46:10) to see them. In the middle of the nineteenth century, Elizabeth Barrett Browning, a young sickly English woman, reminded us of what we often miss. In her beautiful poem "Aurora Leigh," she wrote, "Earth is crammed with heaven and every common bush afire with God, but only he who sees takes off his shoes. . . . The rest sit 'round and pluck blackberries and daub their natural faces unaware." A colorful sunrise happened this morning and too few of us witnessed that miracle. The good news is that there's an early December sunset scheduled this very afternoon. You can't do anything to hurry it up or slow it down. If you want to fully appreciate it, to take in its majesty, to be renewed, don't just do something, stand there!

Be a diamond dealer. Most men and women don't recognize a diamond in its raw state, but a diamond dealer does. Before the rough edges are chipped off and the core polished to a dazzling sheen, these ordinary-looking rocks are easily discarded. John Steinbeck once sat in a fifth-grade class. In that room he was not yet a brilliant writer. Fortunately, a teacher recognized that glimmer of light underneath the tough exterior and chipped away. A few years later when he was awarded the Nobel Prize for literature, he thanked that teacher first. In his acceptance speech, he stated, "What deathless power lies in the hands of such a person!" You can be such a person to your spouse. It is not a difficult task to find faults and blemishes in the sack of flesh your spouse inhabits, but it is very Christian to dwell on the fine good things in others (Philippians 4:8) to recognize those glimmers of hope and beauty that shine through. With a little spit and polish, you'll have a diamond anybody can recognize.

Make mole hills out of mountains. One of the best sermons ever delivered was on the side of a mountain by an itinerate carpenter who knew a thing or two about geography and people. He knew we are prone to fighting over things big and small. Humans tend to be a righteously indignant, war-like bunch, and the natural differences between us present good reasons to fight. To protect ourselves, we hide behind barricades pieced together with bubble gum and petty differences. Given time and mounting disagreements, these blockades become mountains that are difficult to get over for friends and enemies alike. We know that we stand a much better chance of surviving together than alone. Paradoxically though, the more we insist on protecting ourselves with flimsy walls and mountains we've fashioned atop mole hills, the more isolated and vulnerable we become.

Ever the counter-cultural revolutionary, the preacher told his congregation on the mountainside that day to be peacemakers, to do what it takes to get people together. He said those who do will be blessed and recognized as "children of God" (Matthew 5: 1–12). However, to make peace, these children must be coaxed from their hiding places and convinced to tear down the walls and mountains they created. It can be done as it began, with little things. A kind word here, a smile there can help to chip away at even the most imposing mountain. With time and patience, eventually the steepest mountains can transform into mole hills.

Teach new dogs old tricks. I suspect most old-timers know when the Social Security check hits the bank and the early bird special starts at the diner. If that's you, you may feel you're too old to learn new stuff, since you can't teach an old dog new tricks. While some of that may be true, these ideas have been around for a while, and like Crest toothpaste, "have been shown to be effective when used in a consciously applied program." These ideas may have collected a little dust over the centuries, but they still work. Based on the total number of marriages in the United States this year, about 6,200 people will get married today, most of them young people. So if leaving and cleaving makes any sense, share these notions with these young dogs. While it may be impossible to teach old dogs new tricks, you can teach young dogs old tricks.

Invest in a good umbrella. Somewhere in the world, it's going to rain today. The clouds will thicken up, and it may get gloomy, but if you have an umbrella you can go about your business. If you don't have an umbrella, you may be trapped inside. However, it can rain inside also. Ominous, heavy dark clouds can roll in and ruin your day, your parade, and your marriage. Longfellow sounded that warning years ago in "Rainy Day," but he had some good news for those who were ready. He wrote:

> Be still, sad heart! and cease repining;
> Behind the clouds the sun's still shining;
> Thy fate is the common fate of all,
> Into each life some rain must fall,
> Some days must be dark and dreary.

Rainy days are unavoidable, but for those with the right perspective and who previously secured what they value, there are lots of reasons for hope. On dark, rainy days, the blackness can be overwhelming and the only thing we see. It's easy to forget that the sun never quits shining, but to see it for yourself you may have to rise above the clouds and be optimistic. To paraphrase some advice to the people of Philippi, look beyond the clouds and keep your mind on stuff that's lovely, good, true, and worthwhile. Forget the rest (Philippians 4:8). Tomorrow will take care of itself, but for heaven's sake, buy an umbrella and some galoshes and go play.

Choose love. Love is a choice, a verb, something you decide to do or not to do. Each December, we all stand on the edge of a new year that is chock full of surprises—some good, others not so much. Over the subsequent twelve months, some lives will begin and others will end; some fortunes will be won and some lost; and some friendships will begin and others broken. In this sea of change and turmoil stands the constancy of the One in charge. As T.S. Elliot wrote, "There is but one still point in the turning world." Most of the stuff that happens is beyond your control. You're responsible for how you react to these events. As Viktor Frankl reminded us in *Man's Search For Meaning*, our ability to choose our attitude regardless of the circumstance is the single most powerful of human freedoms. It cannot be taken away, but it can be surrendered. Therefore, choose life. More importantly, choose to love the person you have chosen.

THE ENDING

IT IS A DAUNTING AND presumptuous task to take on marriage as a book subject. After all, there are about 62 million married people in America, and most of them know (or think they know) how it ought to work.

In our multicultural society, there is a wide variety of theological, philosophical, and cultural foundations that inform views on this life-changing, "common" experience. As a man of faith, I, too, have a clear bias on how messy human beings join together "till death do us part." Consequently, this book is from the Christian tradition and leans heavily on Scripture for inspiration. However, as an educational psychologist, I know there is common ground across a range of human opinions about how this monumental event begins and ends. I'm not sure one can improve on the elegantly simple 3,000-year-old biblical advice on marriage to leave and cleave (Genesis 2:24). But whatever your faith or cultural tradition, in the question of marriage, it's vital to heed Jean Jaures's beautiful admonition, "From the altars of the past, let us take the fire and not the ashes."

REFERENCES

AI Overview. (n.d.). *How baking powder works*. Available at https://www.google.com/search?q=how+does+baking+powder+work&sca_esv=0da12726fba0ca1f&sxsrf=ADLYWILECk79_EfY7u8FivNA3YRaP1VSFw%3A1736351005274&ei=HZ1-

Anthem Lyrics. (n.d.). Lyrics.com. Retrieved December 5, 2024, from https://www.lyrics.com/lyric/14639893/Leonard+Cohen/Anthem.

Baylor, R. (Editor/Compiler) (1978). *Fine frenzy: Enduring themes in poetry*, 2nd edition. Boston: McGaw-Hill.

Buechner, F. (1993). *Wishful thinking: A seeker's ABC*. San Francisco: Harper.

Cohen, L. (1983). *Hallelujah*. Hipgnosis Song Management, available at https://www.hipgnosissongs.com/

Collins. F. (2007). *The language of God: A scientist presents evidence for belief*. New York: Free Press. ISBN-10: 1416542744

Craig, S. (2012). Laughter is the best medicine. *Patient Care*, August 1. 2021. University of California San Francisco. Available at: https://www.ucsf.edu/news/2012/08/104621/laughter-best-medicine

Duckworth, A. (2016). *Grit: The power of passion and perseverance*. New York: Scribner. ISBN-10 1501111108

Eisenman, R. (2008). Scientific insights regarding the orgasm. *Europe's Journal of Psychology*, 4(2). Available at https://ejop.psychopen.eu/index.php/article/view/430/html

Eliot, T.S. (2001). *Four quartets*. New York: Gardners Books; Main edition. Originally Published 1943.

Felleman, H. (1965). *Poems that live forever. America's favorite poems of love and friendship, humor and whimsey, faith and inspiration*. New

York: Doubleday. ISBN 0-385-00358-7.

Frankl, V. (1997). *Man's search for meaning.* Washington DC: Washington Square Press. ISBN 9780671023379.

Frost, R. (n.d.). *The road not taken.* Retrieved from Poets.org, https://poets.org/poem/road-not-taken October. 2024.

Gibran, K. (1923/1998). *The prophet.* New York: Knopf Publishing. ISBN 0394404289.

Gimein, M. (Ed.). (2022). Why Gates traces roots. *The Week,* November 4, 2022, 22(1103). p. 10.

Gladwell, M. 2007). *Blink: The power of thinking without thinking.* Boston: Bay Back Books. ISBN:978-0316010665.

Greeley, A.M., Michael, R.T & Smith, T.M. (1990). Americans and their sexual partners. *Society* 27. 36-42. Available at https://gss.norc.org/content/dam/gss/get-documentation/pdf/reports/topical- reports/TR17%20(old)%20Americans%20and%20Their%20Sexual%20Partners.pdf

Hite, S. (1987). *Women and love: A cultural revolution in progress.* New York: Knopf. ISBN-10:0394530527.

Illinois State Board of Education. (n.d.). *Cutting edge curriculum: methods of heat transfer.* Retrieved October, 2024 from https://www.isbe.net/CTEDocuments/FCS-700016.pdf

James, W.(2008, originally 1899). *Talks to teachers on psychology: and to students on some of life's ideals.* Boston: Standard Publishing Corporation.

Jong, E. Y. (2016). Therapeutic benefits of laughter in mental health: a theoretical review. *Tohoku Journal of Experimental Medicine,* 239 (3), pp. 243-249. doi: 10.1620/tjem.239.243. Laughter helps…moving mouth upward changes the mood.

Kazantzkatis, N. (2014). *Zorba the Greek.* New York: Simon & Schuster. ISBN-13 978-1476782812

Kearney, M.S. (2023). *The two parent privilege: How Americans stopped getting married and started falling behind.* University of Chicago Press. ISBN-10: 0226817784.

Krebs, D. (2021, July 15). *Poetry Friday: Earth is crammed with heaven.* Blog. Available at https://mrsdkrebs.edublogs.org/2021/07/15/

poetry-friday-earths-crammed-with-heaven/

Kristof, N. (2023, September 13). The One Privilege Liberals Ignore: Opinion. *New York Times*, / On the impact of two parent: Families headed by single mothers are five times as likely to live in poverty as married-couple families.

Krznaric, R. (2013). The ancient Greeks' 6 words for love and why knowing them can change your life. *Yes Magazine*. Available at https://www.yesmagazine.org/authors/roman-krznaric

Lucas, R.E., Clark, A,E., & Diener, E. (2003). Reexamining adaptation and the set point model of happiness: reactions to changes in marital status. *Journal of Personality and Social Psychology*, 84, (3), 527-539.

Machiavelli, N. (2021). *The Prince*. New York: Reader's Library Classics, Incorporated. ISBN 978-1954839274.

National Center for Health Statistics. (n.d.). *Marriage and divorce*. Center for Disease Control. Atlanta. Available at https://www.cdc.gov/nchs/fastats/marriage-divorce.htm

NORC University of Chicago. (n.d.). General Social Survey (GSS). Available at https://gss.norc.org/

Online Dictionary of Etymology (2017). Available at https://www.etymonline.com/

Overstreet, P. & Schlitz, D. (1987). *Forever and Ever, Amen*. Moon Music, Inc.

Peltzman, S. (2024). Is money or marriage the key to happiness. Chicago Booth Review Podcast. June 12, 2024. Available at: https://www.chicagobooth.edu/review/podcast/is-money-marriage-key-happiness

Rosten, L. (1986). *Captain Newman, M.D.* New York: Dell Publishing. ISBN-10 0440110602.

Rothwell, J. (2024). *Married Americans thriving at higher rates than unmarried adults*. Gallup: Wellbeing, March 22, 2024. Available at: https://news.gallup.com/poll/642590/married-americans-thriving-higher-rates-unmarried-adults.aspx#:~:text=The%20General%20Social%20Survey%20documented,enough%20to%20be%20considered%20thriving

Scott, S.B., Rhoades, G.K,, Stanley, S.M., Allen, E.S., & Markman, H,J, (2014). Reasons for divorce and recollections of premarital intervention: Implications for improving relationship education. *Couples Family Psychology*, 2(2): 131-145 doi:10.1037/a0032025. Available at https://pmc.ncbi.nlm.nih.gov/articles/PMC4012696/

Seesengood, R.L. (2019). "Not grudgingly, nor under compulsion": Love, labor, service and slavery in Pauline rhetoric. p. 141-156 in Fiona Black and Jennifer L. Koosed, eds. *Affect and Biblical Studies. Semeia Studies*. Atlanta, GA: Society of Biblical Literature Press, pp.141-142.

Smith, T (1992).A methodological analysis of sexual behavior questions on the General Social Survey. *Journal of Official Statistics*, 8(3). 309-325. Available at https://gss.norc.org/content/dam/gss/get-documentation/pdf/reports/methodological-reports/MR065%20A%20Methodological%20Analysis%20of%20the%20Sexual%20Behavior%20Questions%20on%20the%20GSS.pdf

Smith, T. (2006). *American sexual behavior: Trends, socio-demographic differences, and risk behavior*. National Opinion Research Center, University of Chicago. Report 25. Available at https://gss.norc.org/content/dam/gss/get-documentation/pdf/reports/topical-reports/sextrend042-13.pdf

Smith, T. (1979). Happiness: time trends, seasonal variations, intersurvey differences, and other mysteries. *Social Psychology Quarterly*, 42(1), 18-30. Available at: https://gss.norc.org/content/dam/gss/get-documentation/pdf/reports/social-change-reports/SC06.pdf

The 10 common reasons for divorce in 2024. (2024). Petrelli Previtera, LLC. Available at https://www.petrellilaw.com/the-10-common-reasons-for-divorce-in-2024/

The Holy Bible, Authorized King James Version (1996). Oxford University Press. Available at https://books.google.me/s?id=6Xs7DwAAQBAJ&printsec=frontcover#v=onepage&q&f=false

The Holy Bible, New International Version. (n.d.). Docdroid. Available at https://www.docdroid.net/13669/the-holy-bible-niv-pdf

This day in history, February 14. Valentine beheaded. Available at https://www.history.com/this-day-in-history/st-valentine-beheaded

Watson, J.D. (1968). *The double helix. A personal account of the discovery of the structure of DNA*. New York: Atheneum Press. ISBN 0-451-03770-7.

Whalen, J.R. (2022). The rising cost of getting a divorce. WSJ Podcast. *The Wall Street Journal*, Wednesday, November 9, 2022. Available at https://www.wsj.com/podcasts/google-news-update/the-rising-cost-of-getting-a-divorce/397a6b3b-dddf-4607-a9b5-6eb03b0c1c58

Zhu, C. (2021). *Happy home happy heart*. An Interview by Yale School of Public Health, The Daily Telegraph.

Appendix

EXERCISES, PROMPTS, AND SURVEYS FOR LEAVERS AND CLEAVERS

...the end of all our exploring / will be to arrive where we started / and know the place for the first time.
—T.S. Elliot (1943), from *Little Gidding*

THANK YOU FOR WADING THROUGH my thoughts on two big biblical imperatives for marriage, *Leaving* and *Cleaving*. My study began years ago when I parked my family's beat-up Ford sedan underneath the old oaks at the Ballard Ball Park on a fine summer's evening. It was my first date, but certainly not Jodi's. I clumsily said something, then out of the blue, she leaned over and she kissed me right on the lips! That was also a first for me, if you don't count my old aunts' kisses at the family reunion. But this time, there was no whiff of face powder and Mama wasn't there. In the uncomfortable awkward silence that followed, I had my first lesson on the voltage in human connections and what all the excitement was about. It was terrifying but such a relief to break the ice. It was also a kick in the pants to know that someone outside of my contractually obligated family really liked me. That night I found out why grown men and women might leave the comfort of one family for the scary proposition of building another with only the pledge of a troth to bind them.

The following prompts and exercises are unapologetically intended to stir your thinking and perhaps revisit old emotions that have been forgotten or misplaced. It may feel like getting your garden ready to feed your family, as you turn up what seems to be a crusty old rock in the process. You wash it off and recognize your old cat-eyed shooter, your favorite marble in the whole world. When you wash the dirt off, old, faded memories, feelings, and faces well up and may leak from your eyes. That sort of amazing grace is what I pray you and your honey discover as you till the fertile ground in your own backyard.

With your sweet thing, decide when and which exercise, prompt, or survey is right for you. Just don't attempt all of them in one evening. Spread out the fun, and remember—there are no right or wrong answers. So, be honest.

To get started, you'll need something to write with in your hand, a pinch of willingness in your head, and a big dollop of courage in your heart. This ultimately is your marriage and your life, and the only people who can make it better or fix what's wrong are the two who traded hearts at your wedding altar. Your creator (like it or not), is the third party in your relationship and has already given you his blessing and sent you a note by John as to what all of this time and hard work should yield: "Beloved, let us love one another" (1 John 4:7).

Now, let's jump into the suggestions to make your unique batch of homemade love a little spicier and healthier.

Where Are We & What Do We Do About It?

Improvement must begin with an honest assessment of your current situation. This exercise is intended to assess the current state of your marriage, identify how you would like it to change, and what you are willing to do to get it there.

Directions

For questions 1 and 2, assign an overall rating from 1 (low) to 10 (high), and for question 3 write at least three things you're willing to do to reach your ideal rating from questions 1 and 2. Then share your responses with your partner.

1. In general, how would you rate your marriage today?
2. What rating would you like to be able to give your marriage?
3. What are you willing to do to reach the rating in question 2?

Fessing Up

God's honest truth is that no one is perfect. Secretly, we've known it all along, but some hide it better than others. As one poet put it, "We wear the mask that grins and lies / it hides or cheeks and shades our eyes. / This debt we pay to human guile / with torn and bleeding hearts we smile." The beauty of marriage is that one person has pledged to love you regardless. This exercise is a way of putting your cards on the table and fessing up.

Directions

1. On a scrap of paper, write down five characteristics about yourself that you were aware of on your wedding day that made you a less than desirable candidate for marriage (i.e., impatient, demanding, moody, etc.).
2. Take turns reading your list to your partner. Ask if any of your revelations surprised your partner.
3. On a separate sheet of paper, write down five characteristics about your partner that originally attracted you to him/her and you believed were desirable traits in a marriage partner.
4. Read your list to your partner and explain why you chose him/her, despite being fully aware of the attributes your partner listed in the first list that were less attractive.

Survey of Strengths and Weaknesses:
Directions
Take the survey below page and enter the results on the scoring sheet on the next page. Use the discussion guide at the bottom of the scoring sheet to process what you have learned.

Survey of Strengths and Weaknesses			
Directions: After reading the definitions of each of the four fundamentals as described in the book, please evaluate your and your partner's Commitment, Communication, Understanding, and Submission levels in each section below with numbers 1 (Low) to 10 (High) and using each number 1–10 only once in each section.			
Section	**#**	**Item**	**Rating** 1 (Low) to 10 (High)
A	1	My COMMITMENT to the marriage	
	2	My ability to COMMUNICATE with my partner	
	3	My level of UNDERSTANDING of my partner	
	4	My willingness to SUBMIT to my partner	
		My Average Score for Section A	
B	5	My *Partner's* COMMITMENT to the marriage	
	6	My *Partner's* ability to COMMUNICATE with me	
	7	My *Partner's* level of UNDERSTNDING of me	
	8	My *Partner's* willingness to SUBMIT to me	
		My Partner's Average Score for Section B	

Scoring Directions: Using the numbers in section A & B, compute an average score for each section. Now **put a star** by your and your partner's specific *Strengths* (the highest score in each section) and **circle** the Weaknesses (the lowest score in each section). Discuss the results with your partner. Then together enter all the evaluations from the two surveys in the appropriate blocks on the *Scoring Sheet* and compute those averages. Use the Discussion Guide to reflect on this experience.

Scoring Sheet for Strengths and Weaknesses

Directions: Together, enter the ratings from both surveys (yours and your partner's) in the appropriate block on this Scoring Sheet. Compute the averages in the rows and columns and identify the *Strengths* (the highest average) with a star and by circling the *Weaknesses* (the lowest average). With your partner, use the *Discussion Guide* below to respond to this exercise.

Rating	COMMITMENT to the marriage	The ability to COMMUNICATE with my partner	The level of UNDERSTNDING of my partner	A willingness to SUBMIT to my partner	Average Rating (Rows)
My Rating of Me					
My Partner's Rating of Me					
My Partner's Rating of Self					
My Rating of My Partner					
Average Column Rating					

Discussion Guide

Questions: 1. What did you learn: a. about yourself? b. about your partner? 2. As a result of this learning, what specific things are you willing to do to: a. increase your strengths? and b. shore up your weaknesses?

Prompts: 1. Complete these sentences as many times as you can. a. After seeing these results, it occurred to me that... b. I believe our marriage could be better if I...

Write Your Own Prompt

Carve out some time to spend an hour writing, talking, and listening with your beloved. Start in a room by yourself for fifteen minutes, writing out a list of topics you need to discuss. Then come together and share your lists. One at a time, each partner chooses one item from his or her partner's list to discuss. At the end of the hour, discuss at least one thing each learned in the last hour. Make time to follow up on topics not yet discussed.

Exploring Creative Differences

Grab a big sheet of drawing paper and some markers, chalk, or colored pencils. Sit across from each other and draw your partner, adding lots of color and background. At the end, sign and date your artistic interpretation of your partner and tape it to the wall. Hang the art in a prominent place to remind you that you live with a real masterpiece.

Discovering the Secrets to a Happy Marriage

The overwhelming majority (87% according to Laver) of marriages are "happy." Consequently, if you're seeking a marriage expert in your area, you won't have to look far.

Directions

Interview three (or more) couples who you believe have a happy and successful marriage. Ask each for their top five most important marriage secrets. Compile a list of Top 3 Secrets to a Happy Marriage by removing the duplicates and prioritizing the remainder. Frame that list and hang it somewhere prominent at home.

How to *Show Up* and *Shut Up*

Directions

Like all skills, listening demands a lot of practice. Before starting this exercise, review these characteristics of a good listener, communication codes, and listening skills that help open a "cold, cold heart" and turn up the heat.

I. Characteristics of a Listener

Empathy/Understanding (ability to take another's point of view)

Genuine (same on the inside as you are on the outside)
Respect

II. Communication Codes
Words
Tone of Voice
Body Language
Facial Expressions

III. Listening Skills: The following are skills you can use **when your honey is experiencing a problem**. They are arranged in ascending order of responsibility and commitment on the listener's part.

- **Attending Behavior**: Stop what you are doing, put down everything, unplug the recording/video machine in your head and be present.

- **Silence**: Practice passive listening with accompanying non-verbal behaviors that communicate interest. Keep your mouth shut.

- **Non-Committal Acknowledgment**: Give brief expressions that communicate understanding, acceptance, and empath. Examples: "Uh huh." "Oh?" "Really!" "I see." "No fooling." "MM-hmm." "You did, huh?" "How about that!" "Interesting."

- **Door Openers**: These are invitations for your partner to expand or continue the expressions of thought and feeling. Show interest and involvement with comments, such as: "Tell me about it." "I'd like to hear what you think about…" "Would you like to talk about it?" "I'd like to listen if you'd like to talk."

- **Non-Verbal Observation**: Make sensitive observation of your sweetie's behavior and attempt to understand feelings that are not being expressed verbally. Examples: "You look sad." "You seem upset." "It looks like you're getting nervous about…" "You seem happy about…" "You look like you need to talk."

- **Content Paraphrase**: Put the facts and content of what your partner says into your own words and send it back for fact-checking. Examples: "Let me see if I got this right, you…" "So, you really told him off." "You're saying, if your plan works, then…" "She just keeps going on and on, huh?"

- **Active Listening**: Help your sweetie understand both the thoughts and feelings of his/her communication. Your response reflects what was said out loud and the feelings and context behind those words. Examples: "You sound upset when she uses your..." "You are not pleased with your part in it." "So, you can't figure out what to do next, huh?" "It sounds like you have strong feelings about..."

Telling Stories Out of School

Our stories offer little peeks at who we are. Some of the more personal and hurtful stories get wadded up in strings of rotting sentences deep in our guts. Unless someone cares enough to let us talk that garbage out, it festers in the dark and can threaten healthy relationships. Hearing this rotten stuff is a sacrifice, but it's one that pleases God (Hebrews 13:16). Sunlight is the best disinfectant I know.

Directions

Now that you're ready to listen, find a time when you won't be interrupted and each of you pick one of the non-threatening topics below. Decide who will talk first and who will listen. Here are the assignments for the **Talker** and **Listener**:

- **Listener**: Invite your partner to tell a story about a topic he or she chooses.
- **Talker**: As clearly and honestly as you can, recall the story.
- **Listener**: Only interrupt for clarification. When your partner finishes, check for understanding by retelling the essence of the story, listening for feelings or emotions underneath the words.
- **Talker:** Conclude by telling the listener (as many times as possible), "I knew you were listening to me when you..."

Talking and Listening Topics

- An important lesson I learned from my parent(s) was _____ because...
- One unhappy experience in my childhood was _____ because...
- My happiest teen experience was _____ because...
- As a kid, I dreamed of being a _____ because...
- Looking back, I've changed my attitude toward _____ because...

- ____ is someone who has influenced me toward ____ because....
- A big turning point in my life was_____ because...
- I'm happiest when _____ because...
- I often regret that I _____. Maybe I could have...
- One of my favorite activities on the weekend is _____ because...
- It breaks my heart when I _____ because...
- One of the things I like about my life now is _____because...

Fogging: An Old Idea for Diffusing a "Bow Up"

Feelings get hurt if we feel we've been attacked, shamed, or otherwise humiliated. Even though the wound may not be intended, William James taught us that feelings are facts. So, if we feel attacked, that's our reality. In milliseconds, the body is ready to fight or take flight, ready to rumble or run.

When your partner gets to this point, it's best to get out of the way. She or he is looking to lash out, exorcize the anger, avenge the hurt or embarrassment, and even the score. You just happen to be a convenient target. What you do now is critical. One of the wisest men who ever lived said "a soft answer turns away wrath." (Proverbs 15:1). As you might suspect, it will do no good to point out to your partner the folly of his or her ways or to give your best reasoned argument. The angry person is too busy marshalling forces for the impending cage match. In the Sermon on the Mount, Jesus told the congregation to "Agree with thine adversary quickly while you are in the way with him" (Matthew 5:25). If you value the relationship, listen. As usual, Jesus is right.

Alcoholic Anonymous reminds us that hurt people hurt people, using digs and insults to inflict maximum pain and suffering. Words can be lethal if you play the dangerous Tit for Tat game. But what if you didn't? What if you refused to play along and responded with soft answers and agreed? What if, like a thick gentle fog rolling in off the ocean, you didn't return the screaming volley served in your court. Although the natural inclination is to smash it right back, such escalation can have disastrous results. If you don't play this hateful game, the angry person eventually puts down the racket. Most angry people just want an audience, somebody to listen as they pour out their hateful venom. A loving, committed, strong spouse can hear the bitterness, frustration, anger, and fear their partner has lugged around.

The Fogging Technique for handling potentially hurtful criticism, insults, slights, etc. works like this.

Agree with…
- **The truth** of the criticism.
- **The odds** of the critical event occurring,
- **The basic principle** of criticism.

The idea is to disarm the critic with kindness by listening and validating his or her feelings. Until the steam is released, the critic is not in a place to sensibly talk and listen. However, after a few rounds of hearing what ails your critical partner, the situation is diffused and the two of you can talk it out. Here's how this might work.

Suppose your partner, Sam, has a difficult case at work, and is under a tight deadline. The boss wanders in and makes a big deal of a minor mistake Sam made in earlier paperwork. Instead of defending himself, Sam tamps down his frustration and bitterness. When he finally gets home, he's ready to unload. It could be the cat, the TV, or the nosy neighbor, but you, a successful and consummate copy editor, is the first thing Sam sees. He slams his keys on the table and you (unaware of his terrible day), say, "Be careful honey, you'll scratch the finish." Sam's internal alarm sounds. In his mind, he's been attacked. "This is my house, too, and I'll do what I please!" he shouts. "Besides, you're not my mother! You have no idea about the day I've had!"

The natural inclination is to defend yourself, but you don't. Sam's way too loud, but he's right. It is partly his house. He can do what he wants. You are not his mother, and until now, you have no idea about his day. So in your kindest voice (and this will require all of the Christianity you can muster), you say, "Sam, you're right. This is partly your house, and you can do what you please. I'm also very aware that I am not your mom, and I didn't realize what a lousy day you had at work. But I'd love to hear about it." If you'll try these soft answers, I think you'll find they really do turn away wrath.

The Rules for Fair Fighting

Occasionally we forget what we know and revert to a self-defense posture. When spouses hurl bombs at each other, things escalate quickly. Stock your relationship toolbox with de-escalation tools to help when things fall apart. A few tools to consider include:

- **CONSIDER the cost**: Make a list of at least five reasons why you are willing to work this problem out. Remember the words of the prophet, "Without a vision, the people perish." Make it clear.
- **CONSIDER those involved**: Review the lists you made for Exercise 2 (Fessing Up).
- **CONSIDER the topic**: Fight about one topic at a time and only about inappropriate behaviors, not labors or character flaws. Being rude is not a behavior. It is a label. "Rude" is sticking your tongue out—most of the time. Sometimes, however, that same behavior is perfectly acceptable (in a doctor's office for instance).
- **CONSIDER the setting**: Do not fight where others can hear you, especially children. Often children are the casualties of the verbal shots fired between adults.
- **CONSIDER the fault**: Beware of blame. It is weak and powerless. We tend to blame our own behavior on uncontrollable external events, while we assume the other's behavior is the result of some internal character flaw. Don't do this.
- **CONSIDER the roles**: Decide Speaker and Listener roles before you start talking. The Speaker should talk about behaviors and how you feel when your spouse does them. The Listener should listen and only talk when the Speaker has finished. The Listener should then repeat the list of behaviors you performed and how the Speaker felt when you did them.
- **CONSIDER the other**: When the Speaker agrees that the Listener has properly connected the behavior and feeling, reverse roles.
- **CONSIDER the outcome**: When the fight runs out of steam, make a mutually agreeable plan to fix the offending behaviors. Write the plan down, noting who's going to do what by when.

Always leave the fighting ground with at least one affirmation given and received.

The Bottom line . . . BE CONSIDERATE!!! You are dealing with one of God's favorite babies. God is on record that those who mess with one of his little ones could be in deep water with a rock tied around his or her neck!

Make and Keep a *Get and Give* List

Little surprises can brighten a day and be remembered several times over the years. Just as surely as "little foxes spoil the vine" (Song of Solomon 2:15), little things nourish it. Quoting the words of Jesus, the writer of Acts declared, "It is more blessed to give than to receive" (Acts 20:35), and Scripture tells us the best way to get what you need is to give away what you want (Luke 6:38). Saint Francis of Assisi's ideas on getting and giving are as fresh and timely today as they were over 800 years ago. He prayed,

Lord, make me an instrument of your peace.
Where there is hatred, let me sow love; where there is injury, pardon;
where there is doubt, faith;
where there is despair, hope;
where there is darkness, light;
and where there is sadness, joy.
Oh Divine Master, grant that I may not so much seek to be consoled
as to console;
to be understood as to understand;
to be loved as to love.
For it is in giving that we receive;
it is in pardoning that we are pardoned;
and it is in dying that we are born to eternal life. Amen!

Place checkmarks beside your 10 favorite items to get and circle your 10 favorite items to give. Then discuss!

Item	Item	Item
Household repairs	Telling me a secret	Cuddling
Paying the bills	Summarizing my POV	Massage/back rub
Cleaning	Forgiveness	Initiating sex
Running errands	Laughing together	Touching me affectionately
Help preparing dinner	Listening to problems	Hugging or kissing
Doing dishes	Personal compliments	Responding to sexual advances
Mowing the lawn	Holding hands in public	Shopping together
Caring for pets	Calming me down	Discussing our finances
Gardening	Being nice when I mess up	Planned outings
Planning meals	Apologizing	Having friends over
Putting children to bed	Understanding me when I'm irritable	Sticking to the budget
Disciplining children	Giving me undivided attention	Going out for dinner
Helping with homework	Trying to cheer me up	Family play time (sports, board game, etc.)
Getting babysitter	Getting/giving presents	Visiting family/friends
Starting conversation	Being nice to my friends	Asking my opinion
Asking about my day	Getting/giving compliments	Something else (explain below)
Having long talks	Looking nice (dressing up, etc.)	

What We Know About Ourselves and Each Other

This fun exercise is intended to generate a fun discussion between you and your spouse. Enjoy!

Directions

Read each item and circle only one answer. When done, discuss your answers and reasoning with your spouse. (If you and your spouse both answer in a single book, use different color pens to differentiate your answers.)

The TV family that's most like the family I grew up in is:
a. *Leave it to Beaver*   b. *The Brady Bunch*   c. *The Simpsons*
d. *The Waltons*   e. *This Is Us*

The hardest thing to maintain throughout marriage is:
a. romance   b. passion   c. communication   d. humor

My favorite artist in the following list is:
a. Picasso   b. Mozart   c. Denzel Washington
d. Billy Joel   e. John Grisham

The Spielberg film that best describes my spiritual development is:
a. *Jurassic Park*   b. *Close Encounters*   c. *Schindler's List*
d. *Saving Private Ryan*

The hardest thing for a man to admit is that he is:
a. broke   b. impotent   c. unqualified   e. aging

I am most uncomfortable talking about:
a. dying   b. sexuality   c. relationships   d. feelings

Most women want their husbands to be like the following George:
a. Washington   b. Straight   c. Clooney   d. W. Bush
e. Lucas

If families were motels/hotels, ours would be: a. Hilton
b. Comfort Inn   c. Budgetel   d. Air B&B   e. Holiday Inn

Of the following Pauls, most men would prefer to be: a. Simon
b. the Apostole   c. Chris (Paul)   d. McCartney   e. Newman

The characteristic women value most in a man is: a. looks
b. kindness   c. money/status   d. sense of humor   e. spirituality

Good relationship skills are: a. automatic   b. acquired
c. passed on by parents   d. less important than passsion

Which Beatles song title best describes your notion of romance:
a. "I Want to Hold Your Hand"   b. "Yesterday"
c. "Twist and Shout"   d. "Eight Days a Week"

It's the worst when a man is:
a. sick   b. poor   c. dumb   d. lonely

Most women want to be like: a. Mother Teresa
b. Michele Obama   c. Martha Stewart   d. Taylor Swift

Sex is to a man as _____ is to a woman: a. sex
b. communication   c. commitment   d. love   e. air

My favorite kind of date would involve:
a. candles and a fine cola   b. a country picnic
c. an expensive hotel room d. a dark movie theater

The song title that best represents how I deal with anger is:
a. "Higher Ground"   b. "Keep on the Firing Line"
c. "Silent Night"   d. "Just a Little Talk with Jesus"

The best fathers are: a. attentive   b. mature   c. providers
d. young at heart   e. teachers

If geography described people, I would be most like:
a. the beach   b. the mountains   c. the prairie
d. the rain forest   e. the swamp

The Love Test: Measuring Up to Love's Calling

The New Testament repeatedly warns against excess pride—in who you are, what you do, and your capabilities. Even on the golf course we tend to think we hit the ball longer than we can. That's why sand traps are almost always *short* of the green. I'm fairly sure there will be no perfect score (the bar is ridiculously high), but it's a good thing to remember now and again.

The Love Test

Directions: If you think you're good at love, try this. Put your initials in the first column all the way down. Then read each item with your name and the characteristic of love (e.g., *John is patient.*) and rate your level of agreement with each statement by putting one check in each line (row) under "Level of Agreement." Score your test with the following scale: SD (Strongly Disagree) = 0; D (Disagree) = 1; A (Agree) = 2; SA (Strongly Agree) = 3. Use the rubric at the bottom to interpret your results, or check 1 Corinthians 13 for further instructions.

Your Initials	Characteristics of Love (I Corinthians 13)	Level of Agreement				Row * Points
		0 SD	1 D	2 A	3 SA	
	1...is patient.					
	2...is kind.					
	3...doesn't envy.					
	4...doesn't boast.					
	5...honors others.					
	6...isn't the center of attention.					
	7...is not easily angered.					
	8...doesn't "get even" for old wrongs.					
	9...doesn't gloat when bad things happen to others.					
	10...tells the truth.					
	11...always protects.					
	12...always trusts.					
	13...always hopes.					
	14...perseveres.					
	15...never fails.					

Total Score	Interpretation Rubric	*Total Score
36+	You're a true saint or "in the running" at least. You probably should be performing weddings, or it could be that you might need to adjust your answer to #10.	
26-35	You're not perfect, but the good news is that God tends to use imperfect people...a lot. I think you know how to get better. Go ahead and put a deposit down on the big anniversary venue.	
11-25	It's OK. Few of us pass, but there are lots of opportunities for "makeup work." But you might want to consider postponing the next girls' or boys' night out or at least repent. By the way, don't be surprised to hear that your name came up at the "special unspoken" request time.	
0-10	Sell your car and use the money to buy a comfortable couch and an asbestos suit. You'll probably need both.	

ACKNOWLEDGMENTS

AS THIS PROJECT ROUNDS THE clubhouse turn, I am keenly aware of the many people who helped get it to the finish line. I am deeply indebted to all of them. My thoughts and ideas in this text are reflections of their influence, especially the good parts. I thought up the rest.

In my day job, I trained teachers for a living and reminded them that more is caught in a classroom than taught. We learn from each other and occasionally on purpose. Over the years, I've collected a mountain of evidence supporting that theory, and this book is one more significant data point. Along the way, my teachers have included my students, friends, colleagues, and family. Without lesson plans, visual aids, or social media, they have quietly shown me how real loving human relationships work. Thankfully, I took notes now and then and sometimes even wrote them down. In a real sense, this book is theirs.

Specifically, I would like to thank Daniel Brantley and the editorial team at Argyle Fox Publishing, who offered suggestions and sound advice that made what you have in your hands easier to read and helped me nearly sound like I know what I'm talking about.

I've learned that love comes from a blend of commitment, communication, understanding, and submission from watching Norman and Judy, George and Suzanne, Paul and Darlia, Alan and Trish, Doyle and Lawanna, Ashley and Judy, Bill and Carol, Andy and JoAnn, Lena and Randy (one of my favorite love stories), and so many others. I simply scribbled a few words that attempt to describe what I've witnessed in your lives. *Grateful* is not a big enough word to describe how I feel.

Most of all, I owe everything good in my life to Jodi, my marriage partner for the last fifty-three years. She taught me of love's promises and pleasures and what it means to live loved. I am eternally thankful.

The love overshadowing all of us and wrapping us in a warm embrace, despite our inadequacies and limitations, is the sweet essence of our Creator. Every day in thousands of ways, big and small, the gentle Rabbi reminds us, "Love one another."

Thanks for listening,

Gary L. Riggins